Democracy and the Internet

Leslie David Simon is a senior policy scholar at the Woodrow Wilson International Center for Scholars and the author of *NetPolicy.Com: Public Agenda for a Digital World*. A retired IBM executive, he has written extensively, served as an adviser to the Departments of State and Commerce and to the U.S. Trade Representative, testified before government bodies in the United States and abroad on Internet issues, and chaired numerous industry councils on the subject.

Javier Corrales is associate professor of political science at Amherst College, specializing in the comparative and international politics of Latin America. He was a fellow at the Woodrow Wilson International Center for Scholars in 2000–2001.

Donald R. Wolfensberger is director of the Congress Project at the Woodrow Wilson International Center for Scholars. The author of *Congress and the People: Deliberative Democracy on Trial,* he is a former congressional staff member whose twenty-eight-year career culminated in service as chief of staff of the House Rules Committee in the 104th Congress (1995–1996).

WILSON FORUM

The Wilson Forum series illuminates issues in public affairs with the light of inquiry and experience. These essays reflect on important questions of current relevance through their history, their interplay with economics, politics, culture, and international relations, and their likely future course.

The Wilson Forum series comes from the Woodrow Wilson International Center for Scholars, an institution in Washington, D.C., whose mission is to symbolize and strengthen the interaction between the realms of scholarship and public affairs. The Wilson Forum series draws on authors from both areas and serves a broad audience of readers who share a desire to understand their world and take responsibility for its future.

Democracy and the Internet

Allies or Adversaries?

Leslie David Simon
Javier Corrales
Donald R. Wolfensberger

Edited by
Leslie David Simon

Published by
Woodrow Wilson Center Press
Washington, D.C.

Distributed by
The Johns Hopkins University Press
Baltimore and London

Editorial Offices
Woodrow Wilson Center Press
One Woodrow Wilson Plaza
1300 Pennsylvania Avenue, N.W.
Washington, D.C. 20004-3027
Telephone 202-691-4010
www.wilsoncenter.org   *

Order From
The Johns Hopkins University Press
P.O. Box 50370
Baltimore, Maryland 21211
Telephone 1-800-537-5487
www.press.jhu.edu

2 4 6 8 9 7 5 3 1

Library of Congress Cataloging-in-Publication Data

Simon, Leslie David.
    Democracy and the internet : allies or adversaries? / Leslie David
Simon, Javier Corrales, Donald R. Wolfensberger ; edited by Leslie
David Simon.
        p. cm. — (Wilson Forum)
Includes index.
    ISBN 1-930365-09-8 (alk. paper)
    1. Internet—Political aspects—Case studies. 2. Internet—Political
aspects—Latin America. 3. Internet—Political aspects—United States.
4. Information society—Political aspects—Case studies. 5. Commu-
nication in politics. 6. Democracy. 7. Democratization. I. Corrales,
Javier, 1966–. II. Wolfensberger, Donald R. III. Title. IV. Series.
    HM851 .S555 2003
    303.48'33—dc21   2002009710

Contents

Preface   vii
Leslie David Simon

Chapter 1   Democracy and the Net:
A Virtuous Circle?   1
Leslie David Simon

Chapter 2   Lessons from Latin America   30
Javier Corrales

Chapter 3   Congress and the Internet:
Democracy's Uncertain Link   67
Donald R. Wolfensberger

Conclusion   96
Leslie David Simon

Index   103

Preface

Leslie David Simon

The idealistic technologists who developed the Internet were sure it would reinvigorate democracy and spread democratic values around the globe. They cited many of the Internet's attributes to make their point. The Internet could make everyone a publisher with vast audiences, permitting powerful new modes of free expression. It could build civil society by allowing individuals anywhere to associate with one another in a common cause. It could empower citizens and consumers with new knowledge and tools to challenge government and other large institutions. It could make government transparent and open to scrutiny.

Many of these things are happening. Human rights organizations from Indonesia to Latin America use the Internet to share information and shine a spotlight on repression. When the Milosevic government in Belgrade closed an opposition radio station, the station put its broadcasts on the Internet so that other stations, such as Radio Free Europe and Deutsche Welle, could rebroadcast the programs back to Serbia. Citizens in Egypt read information on the Internet that is censored in the printed press. Governments at all levels in the United

States are placing information online, available to citizens "24/7." We know today that the Internet clearly provides a robust new tool for democracy.

But now we also know that the story is more complicated. The diffusion of the Internet in the early 1990s coincided with the fall of communism and of the Soviet Union. Spreading use of the Internet was contemporaneous with the blossoming of democracy in Eastern Europe, Russia, and parts of Asia. The two phenomena—one technological and one political—became linked in the minds of many people. Perhaps the linkage made us overly exuberant about the Internet's possibilities.

Today we know that there is another side to the story. Those who hate democratic values and human rights have also learned to use the Internet. In the United States and abroad, neo-Nazis and other hate groups maintain Web sites. Terrorist groups like Al Qaeda and Hamas use the Internet to communicate and to recruit new members. The Cuban government spreads propaganda on its own Web sites.

Even more ominously, authoritarian governments attempt to ban the Internet or to degrade its democracy-building features through a variety of means including filtering and censorship, registration of Web sites, regulation of encryption, and criminalization of various forms of Internet use. In China, at least one person has been imprisoned for creating and distributing a list of e-mail addresses.

The first of these phenomena, although frightening, is the less significant. Neither the domestic hate groups nor the international outlaws, whether states or criminal groups, have been able to leverage the Internet's unique characteristics in a way that is nearly equal to their use by legitimate groups. While the Internet may serve them in much the same way as their use of cellular telephones or newspapers, their messages tend to be so far outside the mainstream that they are simply not credible to the great majority of people. Every technology has its illegitimate uses, and the Internet is no exception. Gutenberg's invention of movable type in Europe had an enormous positive impact on the development of Western civilization, even though it has been used over the centuries by villains of all sorts, ranging from anarchist pamphleteers to Nazi Party newspapers. Radio broadcasting was used brilliantly by President Franklin D. Roosevelt to help save American democracy. It was also used by Hitler's propagandist, Joseph Goebbels, for darker purposes.

The second phenomenon—attempts by repressive governments to control the Internet—is more significant and must be taken more seriously. This has become more urgent in the aftermath of the events of September 11. The United States and its allies must learn how to better communicate with the Islamic world, in particular, and must find out whether the Internet, along with other media such as satellite television, can help build democratic institutions there. They must do so in spite of the censorship or banning of the Internet by many Arab governments. To learn how to proceed, the United States and its allies need to get beyond the early generalizations about the Internet and democracy, and to try to understand more specifically what experience now shows. This book attempts to examine the impact of the Internet on democracy in three different types of regimes: the Middle East, the world's least democratic region; Latin America, a region of struggling democracies; and the United States, a strong democracy.

Chapter 1, "Democracy and the Net: A Virtuous Circle?" reviews the specific characteristics of the Net—the constellation of private and public networks glued together by the Internet—that foster democracy. It then examines the Muslim nations of the Middle East, comparing their use of the Net and the degree to which their governments try to control it and the extent to which it contributes to the development of democracy. I conclude that the Net can provide substantial assistance to democratic institutions in the countries that are already democratic or experimenting with some aspects of democracy, such as Turkey, Jordan, Egypt, and Morocco. The United States and the other industrial democracies can provide technical and financial assistance to nurture these efforts.

In chapter 2, "Lessons from Latin America," Javier Corrales takes the discussion to a region of the world where democracy is stronger and gaining ground, but one that suffers from weak democratic institutions. Corrales shows that while the Internet promotes democracy in a variety of ways, its effectiveness in many countries is limited not only by repressive regimes but also simply by lack of Internet access for most people. Corrales argues that so-called intermediate regimes—countries with weak and struggling democracies as in Latin America—stand to get the greatest benefit from the Internet. To do so, they need policies that coordinate the activities of government, the private sector, and civil society to greatly increase public Internet access.

In chapter 3, "Congress and the Internet: Democracy's Uncertain Link," Donald R. Wolfensberger examines the efforts of the U.S. Congress to make use of the Internet and advanced information technology in a variety of ways, including communicating with constituents and running congressional operations. As the world's most visible and important democratic institution, Congress should teach us some important lessons by its successes or failures in making use of the Internet at the very heart of democracy. One of Wolfensberger's most salient conclusions is that the terrorist attacks during September 2001 not only drove Congress into cyberspace much faster than it had planned, but also brought about a victory of democracy over terror through Congress's successful use of the Internet to continue operations during the anthrax shutdown.

Taken together, these chapters draw important conclusions for those interested in the relationship between the Internet and democracy. Most of all, they show that while the Internet's power to influence the course of democracy and democratic institutions varies with regimes, it has democratizing potential everywhere. While oppressive governments attempt to take steps to mute that potential, the democracies have powerful ways to amplify it.

I know my colleagues join me in thanking the Woodrow Wilson International Center for Scholars for supporting our research in this field. My chapter grew out of lectures I gave at the Woodrow Wilson Center in September 2001 and at the Moshe Dayan Center for Middle Eastern and African Studies at Tel Aviv University in May 2001, as well as work done for the National Defense University's globalization project. I'd especially like to thank Rob Litwak of the Wilson Center for his encouragement, Martin Kramer and Josh Teitelbaum of the Moshe Dayan Center for introducing me to their work, and Ellen Frost of the National Defense University for inviting me to participate in NDU's important book project, "The Global Century."

January 2002

CHAPTER 1

Democracy and the Net: A Virtuous Circle?

Leslie David Simon

In May 2001 the Taliban officially banned the Internet from Afghanistan. What did they fear? Clearly, they feared all the characteristics of the Net that its proponents had always identified as strong democratizing influences: freedom of expression and association, globalization, civil society, education, economic development. The Taliban were not alone among the world's dictators to distrust the Internet. From the most closed regimes like Iraq and Cuba to more open ones like China and Iran, authoritarian governments have sought in numerous ways to shut out the Internet or to limit its effects on their populations. What better proof could there be that the Net nourishes democracy?

Moreover, the technological innovations that make the Net possible appear to flourish in an open, democratic climate, and are retarded by authoritarianism. Since national security in coming years will depend more and more on technological and economic power, democracies should become stronger, while nondemocratic regimes should fall further behind. That is not to say the Net will usher in an era of ubiquitous democracy. But the strong positive relationship between the Net and democracy should help both established and fledgling democracies—and make it harder for the dictators to maintain their hold on power.

Nevertheless, the proliferating activities of oppressive regimes aiming to stop or limit the Net's unfettered growth have caused critics to question some of these claims. For example, a Carnegie Endowment paper in July 2001 stated that "many authoritarian regimes are successfully controlling Internet use, while using the medium to both extend their reach and push forward national development."[1] An article in *U.S. News and World Report* put it somewhat differently: "Children living under repressive regimes are not going to know what the real Internet is. They will have access only to a sanitized corner, a bowdlerized subset of the truly World Wide Web."[2]

The events of September 11, 2001, make this question more topical than ever. If the Internet's democratizing powers are needed anywhere in the world, it is in the Islamic nations. According to the latest survey by Freedom House, the Islamic nations are the least democratic in the world, with non-Islamic countries three times more likely to be democratic than Islamic states.[3] Can the Net help to reverse this situation? The answer depends at the outset on whether one believes that the Net can bolster democracies or that it can smother them. Which view of the Net is true? Or is the answer more complex than either? This chapter will examine the relationship between the Net and democracy with a special focus on the nations of the Middle East.

Democratic Origins

The American scholar Daniel Bell, in his classic work *The Coming of Post-Industrial Society* (1973), wrote: "If capital and labor are the major structural features of industrial society, information and knowledge are those of the post-industrial society."[4] At a time when the Internet did not yet exist, and when stand-alone mainframe computers still dominated the information technology industry, Bell understood that the phenomenon of information was taking center stage in the world's key economies and societies.

The Marxist ideologues in Moscow read Bell's work avidly and denounced it loudly and often. They realized not only that these ideas—if true—undermined the basic tenants of Marxism, but also, and even worse, that Bell was absolutely right. Only a decade later, the new Soviet policy of *glasnost* encouraged more press freedom and eroded the Soviet system. By 1989, three years before the Net went commercial, the Soviet Union was dead. One wonders if it would have lasted that long if the Net had appeared a decade or two earlier.

Thus, some people had begun to recognize early on that the information revolution that began after World War II with the proliferation of computers and advanced communications systems would be a powerful and positive force for change. The infiltration of computing and information systems into public and private institutions, together with the new class of educated and pragmatic people who developed and operated them, was bound to help wash away the old ideologies. The additional mystique of anti-authoritarianism that would later be attached to the Internet was important, but was not the beginning of the Net's attachment to democratic ideas. The role of the iconoclastic technologists who developed the early Net is an important factor in understanding why it is viewed as a democratizing force—and how an open society contributes to innovation.

It is a great irony that while the Internet was born as a tool for the U.S. Department of Defense, many of the people who designed it and pioneered the hardware and software innovations that made it possible were themselves intellectual free spirits. Among these were John Postel, John Perry Barlow, Mitch Kapor, and Steve Jobs. These people and others like them lived and worked on or near university campuses such as UCLA, MIT, and Berkeley. Many were steeped in the counterculture of the 1960s and 1970s. They came of age during the hippie era, and their anti-establishment views influenced their technology and business innovations. They established the open architecture of the Net that made it accessible to all. Many believed (and some still do) that the software that was used on the Net should also be free to all. Steve Jobs used a marketing technique for Apple that attacked first IBM and later Microsoft as antidemocratic institutions.

From the ideas of these early innovators came such important institutions as The Well, originally called The Whole Earth 'Lectronic Link and co-founded by Stewart Brand, creator of the *Whole Earth Catalogue*. The Well became the prototype forum on the Net, and demonstrated its value as a tool to promote free expression and freedom of association. Other institutions that shared these values were the Internet Society and the Electronic

Frontier Foundation (EFF), founded by Kapor and Barlow. EFF became a premier defender of free expression, privacy, and the "fair use" doctrine of intellectual property law. Its ideas spread and influenced larger and more mainstream organizations, such as the Association for Computing Machinery.

Perhaps it was no accident that the technological breakthroughs in hardware and software were born in the intellectual ferment and freedom of the campuses in the 1970s. If one asks why the United States dominates the software industry, for example, one has to attribute it at least in part to the atmosphere of openness and free expression at U.S. universities—as well, of course, to another attribute of American democracy, the role of entrepreneurship and the open and competitive marketplace. Some Japanese analysts, for example, have decried the more rigid structure of Japanese education, which they believe has held Japan back in the software field by discouraging individualism and entrepreneurship. Europeans, who have performed better in software than the Japanese, but not as well as Americans, place more blame on their strong entry barriers to startup firms.

Thus, the Net was born with an aura of anti-authoritarian feeling and a sense that it facilitated democratic values such as free speech and freedom of association. In addition, the timing of its rise in popularity—from the late 1980s into the 1990s—coincided with the end of the Cold War and the rise of democracy in countries ranging from Eastern Europe to Latin America. Thus, it seemed to most observers that the Net and democracy went hand in hand. Don Heath, president of the Internet Society, said: "If the United States government had tried to come up with a scheme to spread its brand of capital-ism and its emphasis on political liberalism around the world, it couldn't have invented a better model than the Internet."[5]

Harvard sociologist Seymour Martin Lipset went a step further when he proclaimed, "At the dawn of the new century, the United States finds itself in a position of surprising dominance around the world. It has been a triumph of ideas and values perhaps even more than power."[6] In his view, the symbiosis between advanced in-formation technologies and democratic values produces and projects national power.

The question is whether all this is true, or whether it constitutes what the press came to call "Internet hype." Just as some questioned whether or not there was really a "New Economy," others began to question just how democratic the Internet was, and whether or not it also had a darker side.

The Net's Dark Side

Not surprisingly, a reaction to these positive views be-gan to set in during the late 1990s. Studies by the U.S. Department of Commerce and by international agencies such as the Organization for Economic Cooperation and Development (OECD) began to identify a "digital divide," a gap between information haves and have-nots that was threatening to spread inequality not only within countries but between the richest and the poor-est countries. In a 1998 report, for example, the Benton Foundation and the National Urban League charged that the digital revolution actually aggravated poverty by speeding the loss of jobs in the inner city.[7] Others strongly dispute this.

Egregious violations of privacy appeared in the countries that were most advanced in the use of electronic commerce—and that were, of course, democratic. Some of the worst of these were committed in the United States by government agencies, such as the U.S. Internal Revenue Service, and by state governments, both intentionally and unintentionally.

Hackers began to vandalize web sites, to spread so-called viruses and worms, and sometimes to use "denial of service" attacks to bring down commercial or government sites. Many of these campaigns were carried out by amateur thrill-seekers, but others were politically motivated, and some were sponsored by political groups, terrorists, and perhaps even governments.

Some countries began to crack down on free speech on the Net, by requiring registration of Web sites or by censoring the ability to access certain sites. Some countries, notably China, have criminalized certain Internet activities, and in at least one case, made public in 1999, a person in China was actually incarcerated for distributing lists of names. Even democratic nations began to fear the nature of content on the Net, whether in the form of pornography or violent or racist material, and even the language used. Democracies such as the United States, France, and the United Kingdom flirted with censorship. Meanwhile, new technologies were coming online that had the potential to permit governments to track individual use of the Net, or even to locate a person using mobile devices to access the Net.

Finally, the 2000–2001 stock market crash in so-called dot-com stocks and the slowdown in high technology spending prompted some people to ask how real the New Economy is, and whether the digital revolution makes the overall economy more vulnerable to economic turndowns.

Thus, it is fair to ask the question again: What is the relationship between the Net and democracy? Will countries that promote the use of the Net become more democratic and less authoritarian? Will use of the Net make them stronger economically and technologically, and promote their national security? To answer this, it is important to understand the inherent characteristics of the Net.

Democratic Characteristics

The Net has some peculiar characteristics that are at the heart of its ability to corrode totalitarianism.

1. The first and perhaps the most important is the Net's erosion of borders. Not only do digital bits disregard physical boundaries and political borders as they move along fiber-optic cables or over satellite bandwidths, but the use of packet switching and strong encryption makes it very difficult, time-consuming, and expensive for intrusive governments to monitor citizens' Internet use. As a 1997 RAND Corporation publication pointed out, "Information . . . moves around the world on the wings of energy too small to be sensed without instruments. . . . Information is diffusive; it leaks like a

universal solvent despite great and continuing efforts to contain or restrict its spread."[8]

2. The Net's disdain for borders clearly reduces the overall power of governments to control their citizens in a variety of ways. It is also a major facilitator of the Net's second characteristic: It dramatically increases citizens' ability to "seek, receive and impart information and ideas through any media and regardless of frontiers" (Article 19 of the U.N. Declaration of Human Rights). The world's information resources are available instantly in the privacy of one's home, and the cost of publishing one's views to a wide audience approaches zero. Nay-sayers may argue that the Net also permits nondemocratic and malign forces to freely publish their views as well. True enough. But as the earlier Soviet experience shows, even with a monopoly on information, the Soviet apparatchiks couldn't hide the truth from their people. In an atmosphere of free expression, the truth ultimately emerges.

3. The Net promotes the ability of people to associate freely with others who share their views and interests, regardless of where they are located, and to share information with them, to make common cause with them, and to jointly advance their mutual political or other agendas. As one interesting example, the moribund labor unions in the United States have recently begun to use the power of the Net to let employees express their grievances and communicate with other likeminded people. One can only imagine the uses the Polish union movement, Solidarity, could have made of the Net in the early 1980s. It is this characteristic of

the Net—its facilitation of freedom of association—that dictatorial regimes most fear.

4. The Net limits the ability of all governments to regulate the activities in which their citizens engage, based partly on its borderless nature and partly on its empowerment of individuals. As Lawrence Lessig of Harvard Law School has pointed out: "Borders keep people in and hence governments could regulate. Cyberspace undermines this balance . . . [and] escape from regulation becomes easier. The shift is away from the power of government to regulate and toward the power of individuals to escape government regulation."[9] This property of the Net clearly threatens the established order where, for example, governments exert control by ownership of key economic sectors such as telecommunications. Deprived of these monopolies, governments lose enormous power, not only institutional, but economic and even personal, in the case of nations where the leaders benefit directly from monopoly arrangements and closed markets. Serbia and Indonesia are two that come to mind, as does Syria.

5. The Net makes government organization and powers ambiguous in several ways—including the boundaries within and between governments, and the boundaries between government and the private sector. For example, in international electronic transactions, goods may be produced in one country, warehoused in another, ordered from a server in a third, and shipped to a customer in a fourth. The question of tax jurisdiction in such cases becomes complex at best. The same issues apply to intellectual property laws, consumer protection laws, and court jurisdiction issues. Democracies can cope

with these issues bilaterally or multilaterally, but authoritarian regimes cannot contemplate any loss of sovereignty or power.

Complicating this issue, the governments of the industrial world have already proclaimed that the private sector plays the leadership role in the Net. One can go back almost as far as one wishes in search of an example of any government relinquishing control over such a pervasive development. It is because of American success and dominance in Net technologies that most advanced countries have followed the U.S. lead in calling for private-sector leadership of the Net. This does not bode well for authoritarian governments that still wish to control Net development.

6. The speed of the Net's development and diffusion makes it difficult for any government to cope with, especially those that rely on total central control. The United States has learned this well in an area such as export controls, where it is virtually impossible to keep up with advances in technology in a timely way. While this poses problems for democracies as well as dictatorships, it leaves the democracies with a large advantage. Since the private sector leads Net development, Net deployment proceeds inexorably in democracies—sometimes with messy results, as, for example, when privacy rules lag behind use, or when angry legislators pass laws banning obscenity from the Net, only to have them reversed by courts. Nevertheless, democracies muddle through, their system of checks and balances helping them to avoid major and costly errors.

Totalitarian regimes are in a sense "freer" to make bad decisions. For example, as Fahad Abdullah al-Mubarak, a senior Saudi Arabian businessman, pointed out at a Harvard University conference in 1999, Saudi Arabia has had electronic commerce only since 1998, because the government would not issue licenses for commercial Internet service providers (ISPs) until then.[10] The kingdom now finds itself in the position of trying to catch up.

7. The Net has the power to change the way governments operate—forcing them to reinvent themselves and to become more democratic in the process. How does this come about? In two words: openness and access. Government information online is transparent and easily available to citizens, and it does not have to pass through the filter of a civil servant, who may not wish to divulge information. Thus, governments that have secrets to hide from their citizens are right to fear the power of the Net.

While this phenomenon clearly benefits people in the nations that undertake "electronic government," how will it help people under repressive regimes? The first point is that governments around the world are moving to embrace electronic government because of its tremendous cost savings. In the United States, for example, a food-stamp transaction that costs fourteen dollars to do in person costs less than twenty cents electronically. As governments go online, citizens in those countries will become aware of what other countries are doing online, increasing their skepticism toward their own regimes. Second, even the dictators will face financial pressures to permit certain government transactions online. Those countries that retain nineteenth-century methods of conducting government business will be weakened further, devoting too much of their GNP to inefficient government, further eroding their economic growth and prospects.

Governments are also beginning to use Net technologies to improve democracy directly—for example, putting their voting systems online and permitting citizens to communicate directly with legislators and government officials. Costa Rica, for example, hopes to increase the percentage of citizens voting from 65 percent to approaching 100 percent through the use of electronic voting at the nation's schools. Even Russia is implementing electronic government, with all laws passed by the Duma now placed online.

8. The Net empowers individuals and smaller institutions in an extraordinary variety of ways. As we have seen, citizens are empowered in dealing with their governments. Employees are empowered in dealing with employers by being able to communicate easily with each other outside the corporate structure. Consumers are empowered by online access to price and product information and even by being able to set up bidding for their purchases. The relationship with professionals such as physicians is changing as people are able to easily get complex medical information about their conditions, allowing them to question their doctors more thoroughly and intelligently. Thus, the Net erodes authority generally.

As Robert Keohane and Joseph Nye have pointed out, the information age is also empowering smaller nations and changing the nature of power in international relations.[11] States are now using the "soft" power of information much more effectively to influence and change other nations' behaviors. Propaganda and cultural content can be leveraged on the Internet by even the smallest states—but in the unforgiving court of the Internet's global audience, it must be credible in order to be believed. Despite Serbia's attempts to make its case on the Internet in the past decade, no one believed it.

9. The Net is a great enabler of education—one of the foundations of democracy. One no longer has to be physically in Cambridge, Massachusetts, or in Palo Alto, California, to take classes at Harvard or Stanford. The world's universities, as well as elementary and high schools, vocational schools, and training centers, are all beginning to make their courses and their faculties available online. If we recall that one reason for the success of blacks in South Africa in defeating apartheid was that South Africa had one of the world's largest and finest correspondence universities, which permitted many nonwhites to get a university education, we can see the potential of Internet education.

Thwarting the Net's Democratic Potential

The basic characteristics of the Net appear to add up to a strong democratic bias. However, while democratic governments around the world are adopting policies as quickly as they can to foster the development and use of the Net, dictatorial regimes are working equally fast to control its use. Some use total bans, while others impose regulations, even as they attempt to develop the Net's commercial potential. Many, of course, are conflicted and caught between the Net's economic benefits and its political threat.

China is frequently cited as the prime example of a country torn over Net policy. China's reformers and business leaders understand that the Net is crucial to economic growth; they have gotten policies adapted to contribute to its growth, including a sizable investment in the country's backbone academic and research network and the introduction of private competition into telecommunications, a distinctly non-Marxian concept. China is already the world's third largest Internet market, but less than 3 percent of the population is online.

At the same time, Chinese bureaucrats and Communist Party cadres, along with the police and military, have been responsible for the imposition of registration, censorship, encryption, and other rules. While these laws are difficult to enforce, and are routinely broken by students and others, knowledge of the penalties for breaking the law—including long jail sentences—is a strong deterrent. An example of more brutal deterrence is the regime in Myanmar, which makes it a crime punishable by seventeen years in prison to access the Internet without authorization. Regimes determined to prevent citizens from using the Net at all can clearly do so, simply because of their power to terrorize their citizens.

Malaysia and Singapore are also examples of conflicted countries that are working hard to build electronic commerce while preventing their citizens from using the Net to see those things the regimes feel are offensive—whether political, cultural, or religious. Such censorship is technologically possible, of course, but it is difficult in countries that permit some telecommunications and media diversity and are unwilling to go to extreme lengths to frighten their citizens.

One part of the world that is particularly interesting to examine is the Middle East. In the wake of the attacks of September 11, 2001, the question of whether the Internet can help democracy grow in this region is of particular importance.

The Net in the Middle East

The Islamic countries of the Middle East have been slow to use the Internet. The main causes include weak economies, the lack of disposable income, the dominance of English on the Internet (at least until very recently), poor telecommunications infrastructure, and the fear of many governments that Internet access would undermine state control and Islamic culture and religion, which has led to strong censorship.

But now, some catching up is going on. Electronic commerce in the Middle East increased more than tenfold from 1997 to 2000, and reached almost $100 million by the beginning of 1999.[12] As Internet service providers have come online in some countries over the last two or three years, and lowered access costs, the number of users outside Israel has reached 3.5 million people—primarily from the United Arab Emirates, Jordan, Bahrain, Kuwait, and more recently Saudi Arabia. Internet access is growing at a rapid rate and is expected to reach 10 million to 12 million by the end of 2003, according to Nua Internet Surveys. This is still very small, considering there are now at least 500 million Internet users worldwide. Language use is another indicator: Arabic, Turkish, and Farsi account for less than 1 percent of Internet language use; in contrast, Korean accounts for 3.6 percent, and Dutch, 2 percent.

Late in 2000, however, the inaugural meeting of the Arabic Internet Names Consortium in Dubai set up an Arabic-character Internet URL address system. Since then, more than 75,000 Web sites have registered under the system. This should boost total Internet usage even faster, to more than 30 million people by 2005, with the percentage of those users with a knowledge of English dropping from almost 90 percent last year to under 60 percent in 2005.[13]

A quick snapshot by country shows the problems and the opportunities:

Gulf states   Not surprisingly, the Gulf states lead in Internet usage. The United Arab Emirates (UAE) is the most wired country in the Middle East outside of Israel and provides a benchmark of sorts. It has more than 660,000 users and a penetration rate of about 24 percent, placing it twenty-second in the world in percent of users, ahead of France and Spain. There are numerous cyber-cafés (incidentally, a chief spreader of the Internet in many developing countries and an important small business opportunity). But the UAE also censors users by requiring that all Internet access take place through its state-owned monopoly telecommunications carrier, the Emirates Telecommunications Corporation, which filters out certain sites through the use of proxy servers and content managers. The UAE government states that it only filters pornography. The government of Bahrain may also spy on its citizens' e-mail. One Bahraini has spent over a year in jail, according to Human Rights Watch, for e-mailing political information to dissidents abroad.[14]

Bahrain follows the UAE, with 16.7 percent of its population online; Qatar has 10.3 percent; and Kuwait, 8.3 percent. In comparison, Lebanon is at 6.6 percent. All others are less than 5 percent. The UAE also has the lowest number of users per account (three), meaning that many people have their own accounts. Jordan, where people tend to use cyber-cafés rather than have their own accounts, has six users per account; Egypt, where users tend to be university students who log in at school, has eight users per account.

Jordan   In contrast to the UAE, Jordan has experienced strong Internet growth without censorship since 1995. Jordan has six ISPs, although the cost of using them is high: about seventy dollars per month, including telephone charges. This is partly because of high taxes on telecommunications. The most recent estimate of users in Jordan was about 30,000 people. But there are many cyber-cafés in Amman and elsewhere, so people who cannot afford services at home can still use the Internet. Jordanians converse openly on the Internet about subjects barely covered in the press. There are also reports that citizens of other Middle East countries who wish noncensored access dial up and use Jordan's ISPs. Some Jordanian government departments also invite users to visit their Web sites and post comments and questions.

Turkey   Turkey opened to the Internet in 1993 with the ISP Turknet. The Turkish government has been very aware of the benefits of electronic commerce to businesses such as textile producers. As a result, there are more than 200,000 users in Turkey, three-quarters of whom access the Internet via private ISPs. Turkish newspapers are now publishing online editions, and there appears to be no censorship, despite strenuous efforts by groups such as Human Rights Watch to find it. In June 2000, though, the Turkish government did declare that Web sites would be subject to the same censorship as print media.

Saudi Arabia   Saudi Arabia did not establish its own ISPs until 1999, to give the government time to devise means of censorship. Until then, Saudis could only get access by using foreign service providers in countries such as Bahrain, although the high cost of overseas telephone connections impeded use by anyone other than some businesses and research institutions. Today there are about 500,000 users. The Council of Ministers has formed a permanent standing committee that oversees Internet use, including, first and foremost, protecting Saudi society from material that violates Islamic traditions and culture. It is known that the committee has banned more than 200,000 Web sites. Moreover, the Saudi proxy server sends an ominous warning to users trying to access blocked sites.

Syria   Ordinary citizens in Syria were permitted access to the Internet only recently, although Syria has had a connection for official use since 1997. A handful of Syrians use foreign ISPs in Lebanon and other countries, and cyber-cafés are now proliferating.

Morocco   Morocco has seen a growth in local Internet service providers since 1995, and competition has lowered costs to about twenty dollars per month, plus phone charges of about two dollars per hour. Morocco has about 40,000 users, and the government does not restrict access or censor content. There are numerous cyber-cafés.

Libya   Libya began to permit Internet access only in 2001, and Tripoli has a number of cyber-cafés.

Tunisia   Tunisia has allowed private ISPs since late 1997. While the number of users is small (estimated at about 10,000), there are eight providers, six for government, university, and school use and two for private companies and individuals. Late in 1998 Tunisia also took the step of opening twelve Internet access centers, called Publinet, and plans to open eighty-eight more. These facilities are paid for half by the government and half by the Tunisian Development Bank, and are part of Tunisia's effort to become a telecommunications hub for North Africa. Access at these facilities costs about $4.25 per hour. Additionally, Tunisian law requires that ISPs submit the names of their clients to the government.

Iran   Iran made Internet news in the spring of 2000, when it closed 450 Internet cafés offering broadband access. It left open the 1,200 cafés that connect at slow speed. Authorities claimed the cafés had no licenses, but there was no such legal requirement. The reason may have been more mundane. Young people were using the fast lines to make free international telephone calls, and the state-owned telecommunications carrier had seen its revenues drop. Nevertheless, in a country with about 330,000 Internet users (a figure expected to grow to 1.2 million by year-end 2003) there is still a debate over the cyber-cafés and ISPs, and how they should be allowed to connect.

Iran has an advanced Internet infrastructure, with two gigabyte connectivity services in more than 180 towns—

made possible by satellite service provided by Eutelsat and others. Iran filters Web sites; censorship policies are decided by the Ministry of Culture and Islamic Guidance. Like Turkey, Iran recognizes the commercial and cultural importance of the Net. It has even designated the island of Kish as a future electronic city with ample fiberoptic and satellite links. Moreover, a computer institute in Qom has made 2,000 Islamic documents available online, along with the complete works of the Ayatollah Khomeini.

Iraq   Iraq lost much of its telecommunications infrastructure in the Gulf War so that there is little Internet service in most of the country, and no private service but some cyber-cafés. There are reports that north of the Thirty-third Parallel the Turkish backbone is being extended into the Kurdish north, with international telephone calls over the Internet available at very low cost.

Middle East Lessons

What can be learned from these countries' experiences? First, in terms of usage, Internet penetration is growing rapidly, after a slow start, for reasons that range from a more open approach to ISPs by governments, to more use of Arabic on the Net. However, continued government control over both media and content continues to be a drag on growth. The protection of state-owned telecommunications monopolies is a major reason, both to protect the financial elites that benefit from the monopolies and to protect the jobs of thousands of workers who would temporarily face the loss of their jobs due to new competition. Government control over content is another factor.

The region divides into three types of states:

- States that recognize the economic benefits of the Internet and have allowed it to develop freely. These include Jordan, Egypt, Turkey, Morocco, and Lebanon.
- States that are so fearful of the political potential of the Internet that they have elected to forego its economic benefits by essentially banning it or severely limiting its use. These include Iraq and Afghanistan, with Syria and Libya beginning to liberalize.
- Conflicted states that want to enjoy the Net's economic benefits but still control content to protect themselves from its political and cultural openness. These include Saudi Arabia, the Gulf states, Iran, Yemen, and Tunisia.

Clearly, the Internet can have the greatest potential impact on the course of democracy and economic growth in the first category. Not only is the Internet basically open, but to one degree or another, these countries already have some democratic institutions, with Turkey, of course, far in the lead. The Internet will also help these countries develop economically and promote their civil-society sector, which in the long run promotes democratic institutions.

There are already examples of this taking place: Human rights organizations in Egypt disseminate information online. Banned newspapers in Egypt, Jordan, and Algeria can be read online. Citizens of these countries converse regularly with Israelis in chat rooms. As mentioned, the transparency of Jordanian government departments will grow as they go online.

The second category of countries will become relatively weaker with regard to the rest of the world, as they have basically chosen to remain outside the global economy. As productivity increases in nations outside their borders due to the use of advanced technology, they will slip further behind. Oil revenues and military spending will tend to balance and mask the weaknesses somewhat, but cannot sustain these regions forever.

It is in the last category of conflicted countries that the biggest questions arise. The conflicted nations of the Middle East are not alone; countries such as China, Malaysia, and Singapore have also opted to use the Net for its economic potential, but to use censorship and other controls to isolate their people from world news and opinions.

Who will win the technology race: the government censors and political monopolists, or the students and business people who want to make the most effective and open use of the Net? I will place my bets on those who want to open the Net. One amusing example is provided by the government of Yemen, which allows use of the Internet but censors it. Censoring is done by the government ISP, Teleyemen, using the commercial program Surfwatch—a product not exactly designed to thwart democratic development.

The question of content itself is also worthy of some study. While users in Middle Eastern countries can be exposed to ideas and opinions from around the world, thus theoretically countering government propaganda, as we know happened in Eastern Europe, they can also view the Web sites of terrorist organization such as Al Qaeda, Hamas, Hezbollah, or Islamic Jihad. Groups bent on terror or subversion also use the Net to organize and keep in touch with each other. In March 2002, for example, it was widely reported that remnants of Al Qaeda were using e-mail to help them regroup.

The Net also has the potential to be used as a tool for warfare. In the Israeli-Palestinian conflict, Palestinians dubbing themselves "e-Jihad" have organized denial of service and other attacks on Israeli Web sites, attacking eighty sites on December 29, 2000. Not surprisingly, Israeli hackers have struck back. An article in the *McGill University International Review* charged that e-Jihad has links to Osama bin Laden and is merely a regional rehearsal for major cyber-attacks against the west.[15]

The June 1999 report, "The Internet in the Mideast and North Africa," by Human Rights Watch provides an excellent summation of censorship and regulatory Net practices by Middle Eastern countries. It concludes: "In a region where torture is commonplace and free elections the exception, the issue of Internet speech may seem low on the human rights agenda. . . . But it is arguably in . . . more repressive countries that the Internet can have the greatest impact. Wherever it is accessible, the Internet has provided dramatic new possibilities for people to obtain and exchange information locally and internationally. It has been hailed by many as a force for eroding authoritarian political control and aiding participatory democracy."[16]

Future Directions

The obvious question now is what the world's democracies can do to strengthen the Net's democratizing potential in areas like the Middle East, as well as to limit its darker potentials inside their own borders. There are areas of direct assistance, as well as areas where the advanced nations can set an example. Among the key issues are universal access, privacy, security, content, and education.

Universal access The advanced countries should announce goals of 100 percent access for their own citizens and contribute to programs like those of the World Bank and the United Nations Development Program to assist developing countries with test beds that provide public Internet access points. The decision by the Group of Eight at its 2000 Okinawa meeting to create a "Dot Force" to help developing countries by providing technical assistance as well as financing of test projects was a good one. Universal access can be achieved by a combination of market forces—competition and lower prices—and government and private-sector programs targeting schools, libraries, and other public spaces, where access can be made readily available to the public.

Privacy Government intrusion into people's lives is a significant tool for dictators. But privacy is not such a simple issue that any government can simply pass an omnibus law, appoint some monitors, and expect thereby to safeguard citizen concerns. Rather, privacy must be addressed by both the public and the private sectors. The public sector needs to provide an overall framework of principles as well as legal privacy protection to the most important areas, such as government surveillance and financial and medical records. Government also must strongly prod the private sector, through trade, industry, and professional organizations, to develop its own privacy codes and methods of enforcement.

Security   Government must work with the private sector to improve Net security both within and outside the government. The President's Commission on Protecting Critical Infrastructure has provided a good framework for this, and many of its recommendations are being implemented.[17] Government, of course, must protect its own systems, especially those involving national defense, and must improve law enforcement capabilities. In the United States the December 1999 Defense Science Board report on globalization and security also provided recommendations in this arena that are being implemented by the Department of Defense.[18]

Content   It is clear that societies that nurture free expression also promote scientific and economic progress. Nations that wish to excel in Net development must permit free expression and reject censorship. However, free speech requires responsibility and self-restraint on the part of the private sector in order to maintain democratic balance. Nations that find themselves awash in pornography, violence, and racism in their media, including the Net, will ultimately lose their free speech rights, as the political backlash mounts.

Education and human potential   The Net will develop most effectively in those nations that afford their populations the best environment to develop their full potential, including work skills, through education. The democracies must bring their own educational systems into the twenty-first century and assist the developing world to do the same.

The Net and the high technology that surrounds it are potent democracy builders. But they are far from a cure-all. Despite the existence of the Net, the world continues to face challenges of evil and aggressive regimes, terrorism, ignorance, and poverty. The Net will not cure these problems.

But as David Gompert, former U.S. State, Defense, and White House official, wrote in a 1998 paper for the National Defense University, "Information technology is the sine qua non of both globalization and power. . . . It is integrating the world economy and spreading freedom, while at the same time becoming increasingly crucial to military and other forms of national power." Authoritarian regimes, he said, "will be unable to withstand pressures for both political and economic freedom if [they are] to achieve technological success and integration into the world economy."[19]

In other words, two paths are open to the tyrants. They can become more open and democratic, and advance their power and national economies. Or they can resist change and fall further behind the new virtual and more powerful democratic world. The democracies benefit in the long from either scenario, but let us hope that countries choose the path of openness and democratization.

Notes

1. Shanthi Kalathil and Taylor C. Boas, "The Internet and State Control in Authoritarian Regimes: China, Cuba and the Counter-

revolution," Carnegie Endowment working paper, Washington, D.C., July 2001.

2. Randell E. Stross, "Digital Domain," *U.S. News and World Report,* 26 November 2001, 47.

3. "Freedom in the World 2001–2002," Freedom House, New York, 18 December 2001.

4. Daniel Bell, *The Coming of Post-Industrial Society* (New York: Basic Books, 1973).

5. Steve Lohr, "Welcome to the Internet, the First Global Colony," *New York Times,* 9 January 2000, Section 4, 1.

6. Seymour Martin Lipset, "Still the Exceptional Nation," *Wilson Quarterly* (winter 2000): 31.

7. The Benton Foundation Web site, <www.benton.org>, as well as a subsidiary site, <www.digitaldividenetwork.org>, provides a wealth of information on the question of universal access and the digital divide.

8. Brian Nichiporok and Carol Builder, "Social Implications," in *In Athena's Camp,* ed. John Arquilla and David Ronfeldt (Santa Monica, Calif.: RAND Corp., 1997), 296.

9. Lawrence Lessig, *Code and Other Laws of Cyberspace* (New York: Basic Books, 1999), 207.

10. Remarks of Fahad Abdullah Al-Mubarak, "The Jedda IT Forum on E-Commerce," Harvard University Information Infrastructure Project, Cambridge, Mass., October 1999, 9.

11. See Robert Keohane and Joseph S. Nye, Jr., "Power and Independence in the Information Age," *Foreign Affairs* (September–October 1998): 81–94.

12. Country and regional statistics for the Middle East tend to lag and to be inexact. Official sources, when they exist, are not always reliable, and international organization sources, such as the International Telecommunication Union, tend to be out of date. For this chapter, I have used a variety of sources, including Nua Internet Surveys, Forrestor Research, the Pyramid Research Group (a division of the Economist Intelligence Unit), Ajeeb.com, and the Harvard Information Infrastructure Project.

13. Pyramid Research Advisory Service, Cambridge, Mass., 19 April 2001, 1–2.

14. "The Internet in the Mideast and North Africa: Free Expression and Censorship," Human Rights Watch, New York, June 1999, 42.

15. Hanson R. Hosein, "Bytes without Blood: Virtual War in the Middle East," *McGill University International Review* (winter 2001): 7.

16. "Internet in the Mideast and North Africa: Free Expression and Censorship."

17. *Report of the President's Commission on Critical Infrastructure Protection* (Washington, D.C.: Government Printing Office, 13 October 1997).

18. Office of the Undersecretary of Defense for Acquisition and Technology, *Final Report of the Defense Science Board Task Force on Globalization and Security* (Washington, D.C.: Government Printing Office, December 1999).

19. David C. Gompert, *Right Makes Might: Freedom and Power in the Information Age,* McNair Paper 59 (Washington, D.C.: National Defense University Press, May 1998), 5–6.

CHAPTER 2

Lessons from Latin America

Javier Corrales

As the Internet revolution began, analysts reacted with either excessive enthusiasm or excessive trepidation. Cyber-enthusiasts expected the Internet to revolutionize, not just our economies, but also our politics.[1] The Internet would empower the political Davids (common citizens, neighborhood associations, repressed minorities, underrepresented groups) and restrain the Goliaths by making their actions easier to scrutinize. The cyber-phobes imagined nothing less than an Orwellian nightmare of Big Brother using the Internet to invade personal privacy.

In OECD countries at least, more than a decade after the invention of the World Wide Web, the fears of the cyber-phobes have not materialized, but neither have the impressive gains predicted by the cyber-enthusiasts.[2] Few major transformations in politics seem to be occurring.[3] The bursting of the dot-com bubble in 2002 further dampened the mood of cyber-enthusiasts. Those who once expected dot-coms to revolutionize democracy now feel embarrassed at their hyperbole. Cyberphobia and cyber-enthusiasm seem to be giving way to cyber-skepticism—the belief that the Internet has a minimal effect on democratization, after all.

However, the reason that the outcomes in OECD countries have fallen short of expectations is that the arguments about the political effects of the Internet have ignored differences in political regimes. This chapter argues that the democratizing impact of the Internet varies according to preexisting degrees of democratic development. In countries at either end of the spectrum—either highly democratic or highly undemocratic—the democratizing effects of the Internet are likely to be modest. In these countries, political institutions and avenues of participation are either too strong or too hermetically sealed to be seriously affected—one way or another—by the rise of a new technology.

In intermediate regimes, in contrast, the Internet is likely to have a more noticeable democratic impact. These are regimes whose political institutions are formally democratic, but seriously defective: party systems are volatile, political parties and parliaments lack technical expertise, the judiciary lacks independence, horizontal checks on power are fragile, rights are inconsistently enforced, freedom of the press is informally curtailed, financial donors have excessive influence over public policy, etc.[4] It is in these regimes that the Internet can make the most difference. Citizens in these regimes have more incentives and freedoms to use the Internet to monitor the government than governments have to monitor citizens. The Internet might not create or destroy democratic institutions, but it may soften the imperfections of existing institutions and help citizens cope with them.

The democratizing impact of the Internet also varies according to type of citizens. Fully enfranchised citizens, enjoying not just political and civil rights, but also economic and social rights, are least likely to feel the democratizing impact of the Internet. Less enfranchised citizens are more likely to profit politically from the Internet.

The democratizing potential of the Internet in intermediate regimes and on second-class citizens is a crucial reason for studying the conditions that give rise to the expansion of Internet connectivity in developing countries. *Internet connectivity* is defined as the degree to which citizens have access to the Internet and the ways they use it. Access and usage can vary across regimes and across groups within regimes. A second purpose of this chapter is to offer some insights about the factors that propel Internet expansion.

Market forces are a necessary but insufficient ingredient for full Internet connectivity. They alone will not correct the fact that Internet connectivity in most developing countries remains low and obviously class-biased. While Internet connectivity is inconceivable in the absence of market forces, economic liberalization will not solve the fundamental political obstacle to Internet expansion: namely, the need for a *coordinating agent*. The private sector in most developing countries will simply not make the necessary investments without coordination—that is, without a third party ensuring that the other involved actors make complementary investments. Expanding the Internet requires solving this coordination dilemma, and the state is the actor best suited to do so.

In this chapter, I offer some hypotheses about which states are more likely to undertake such a coordinating role, based on a comparison of incentives facing authoritarian and democratic regimes. While some authoritarian regimes might be more motivated than democratic regimes to expand the Internet, their natural fear of information will always hold them back. Democratic states might not necessarily decide on their own to launch a vigorous drive to promote the Internet. But because they don't fear information to the same degree as authoritarian states, they can be much more easily persuaded by nonstate actors to do so. This explains why market-oriented democratic states are more likely than others to expand the Internet.

Internet connectivity ought to be considered as a cause, as well as an outcome, of democratization. In the parlance of statisticians, Internet connectivity ought to be seen as both a dependent and an independent variable of democratization. The Internet is more likely to expand where there are greater levels of political and economic freedom, and once introduced, it is more likely to enhance democracy among those regimes with intermediate levels of political freedom.

Internet Connectivity and Democracy

The case for the Internet's democratizing potential can be summarized in two words: information and coalitions. The notion that information is a force for democracy has a long lineage in contemporary political science, dating back to modernization scholars such as Seymour Martin Lipset, who theorized about the democratic payoffs of citizens' access to the media.[5] The Internet takes this promise further. It liberates citizens from the information constraints that historically hindered the monitoring of political abuses. The Internet makes it harder to control or hide information. For instance, when then vice president Al Gore was about to deliver his first concession speech on November 8, 2000, an aide monitoring a Florida election Web site discovered that Texas Governor George W. Bush's lead had suddenly shrunk to a few thousand votes.[6] Gore accordingly abandoned his plans to concede, ushering in a reexamination of the Florida voting that, in the end, revealed irregularities in the voting process.

The Internet may not necessarily increase citizens' appetite for political information and activity.[7] Nonetheless, it lowers the obstacles to grassroots mobilization and organization, which in turn empowers interest groups that are further from the mainstream, in a process that Bruce Bimber calls "accelerated pluralism."[8] The Internet has also been shown to increase voting turnout without compromising the security of the vote.[9] The Internet allows citizens worldwide to form cybercoalitions, which hold the promise of liberating citizens from geographical constraints on collective action. It also potentially liberates citizens from having to rely on the state to act as an intermediary in their relations with external actors.[10] And while it is true that the Internet can empower abusive governments, computer-literate users can "hide" from the government through the use of "anonymizer devices" that ensure privacy.[11] Internet connectivity can empower citizens and disenfranchised groups more than it empowers authoritarian governments.

Several counterarguments can be raised against treating Internet connectivity as a democratic force. One is that Internet connectivity is just a subcomponent of other, more commonly accepted standards of democracy. For instance, some might argue that engaging with others through the Internet is nothing more than old-fashioned "civicness," or that the capacity to monitor the state is nothing more than what political scientists now label as "accountability."

There is no question that much of what citizens can do over the Internet overlaps with existing democratic requirements. Yet there are Internet activities that cannot be classified easily under traditional components of democracy. For example, when supporters of presidential candidate Ralph Nader used the Internet to swap votes in the 2000 presidential elections in the United States, they were not exactly forming civic associations or maximizing vertical accountability.[12] Instead, they were uniquely using Internet technology to avoid wasting their votes. Internet connectivity permits political activities that might overlap with, but are not entirely subsumed under, traditional democratic practices.

Another reservation about treating Internet connectivity as an independent requirement of democracy focuses on the "ugly side" of the Internet. The Internet, many warn, could exacerbate political maladies: the already powerful can exploit the Internet to their advantage, while the have-nots remain ill equipped to profit from it.[13] Authoritarian regimes can employ the technology that OECD governments are using to regulate illegal Internet activities (such as filtering and user-tracking devices), in order to monitor the activities of dissidents and to block information. Criminal activities can flourish over the Internet. Stories that Osama Bin Laden disseminates instructions to members of al-Qaeda by hiding messages in the Internet, possibly in pornographic Web sites, circulated in Washington shortly after the September 11 attacks.[14] The Internet could become captive to a few multimedia giant corporations, becoming a source of "standardized," nondiversified information. It could also become a source of packaged entertainment rather than politics-related news, and could serve as an incentive for solitude rather than civic engagement.[15] Citizens could be reduced to mere clickers, civic activism could become mere screen voyeurism, and political giants could use the Internet to undermine the privacy of everyone else.[16]

Yet many other standards of democracy suffer from the same ambivalence, and we do not exclude them as benchmarks for democracy. For instance, social movements may enhance democracy, but by themselves, they do not ensure democratic transition and consolidation. Participation fortifies democracies, but it is also a favorite tool of many totalitarian states. Even elections can be manipulated to serve the interest of dictators. That Internet connectivity can play dual roles should not disqualify it as a democratic standard either.

Rather than excluding Internet connectivity from our list of democratic requirements, we should include it. We should also embrace a broader conception of Internet connectivity. In addition to access, it is also important to obtain data, not just of usage, but also of ownership and control of Web sites and hardware—that is, whether actors use the Internet to advance the public interest or to undermine it.[17] In China, for instance, the government restricts control by requiring citizens to use government-sponsored servers. In every country, the Internet is used to promote criminal activities, terrorism, and violence. These restrictions and abuses of the Internet constitute violations of democracy that would not be apparent if we look at access levels only. The problem is that forms of control and usage are harder to quantify than access, and for that reason this chapter examines mostly the role of access.

Internet connectivity is not a democratic panacea. High levels of connectivity alone will not bring a country to the endpoint of its democratic potential. Democracy is clearly more than just having more information or more allies. But the Internet permits new and different forms of citizen empowerment. Internet connectivity ought to be considered a new standard that regimes must meet to qualify as democracies.

Enhancing Democracy: Intermediate Regimes and Second-Class Citizens

An appropriate site to explore the effects of the Internet is Latin America because it is the quintessential intermediate-regime region. Although it has achieved the highest levels of civil and political rights of any developing region, Latin America's democratic institutions are plagued by problems.[18] Latin America is among the worst performers in the world in terms of respect for the rule of law, degree of corruption, effectiveness of public agencies, and propensity toward political gridlock.[19] In many countries, parties are neither strong enough to act reliably, nor weak enough to disappear and make room for new forces. Precisely because institutions are neither strong nor weak enough, Latin America is ideally situated to benefit from the democratizing potential of the Internet—perhaps not as much as cyber-enthusiasts predict, but certainly far more than cyber-skeptics would argue.

Based on the crudest measure of Internet connectivity—access—it is clear that the Internet revolution is in full swing in Latin America. Between 1994 and 1999 the number of Internet users climbed almost eighteenfold (from half a million to nine million), far outpacing the region's economic growth rate.[20] The number of Internet host computers grew faster in Latin America than in any other region in 1999, making Latin America the fastest-growing Internet market in the world (see table 1). The wireless revolution has made even deeper inroads.[21] The number of cell phone subscribers in Latin America soared to 39 million in 1999, up from just 100,000 in 1990.[22]

The Internet is starting to show its democratizing potential, or at least, its potential as an effective transmitter of political information.[23] Newspaper Web sites are among the most visited sites by Latin Americans. Internet users in Brazil express greater confidence in "their capacity to influence this country's politics" than nonusers.[24] Peruvian citizens with access to the Web site of

Table 1. The Telecommunications Revolution in Latin America

	Percent of Countries That Have Privatized National Tele-communications by 1999	Percent of Countries That Allow Competition in Basic Tele-communication Services	Growth in Internet Hosts in 1999
Americas	70	36	136*
Africa	28	14	18
Arab states	33	15	N/A
Asia-Pacific	46	23	61
Europe	55	39	30

Source: ITU, "Americas Telecommunication Indicators" (Geneva, ITU, 2000).

* Includes Latin America only. The percentage of North America is 74.

Argentina's largest newspaper (www.clarin.org) were able to listen to presidential candidate Francisco Toledo and writer Mario Vargas Llosa discuss how President Alberto Fujimori was trying to rig the May 2000 elections. The information disseminated by the Internet, among many media, possibly deterred Fujimori from claiming victory in the first round of elections.[25] In Venezuela, when the semi-authoritarian president Hugo Chávez began to harass the daily *El Nacional* in 2001, hits of the newspaper's portal surged, registering the record number of 2 million pages visited per day.[26]

Argentines have responded to the depression of 2001–2002 by flocking to the Internet. When the government froze bank deposits, hundreds of neighborhood assemblies *(asambleas barriales)* emerged in protest. They created their own Web site (www.cacerolazo.com), which allowed approximately 180 assemblies to coordinate their activities and post their demands.[27] By 2002 officials in the city government of Buenos Aires were receiving more than four hundred e-mail messages a day to complain or to demand a service, and some of these officials were spending at least an hour a day responding to those messages.[28]

The Internet has also made possible the rise of transnational cyber-coalitions. The most notable example is the Chiapas rebellion in Mexico. Although the rebel leaders embrace an antiglobalization rhetoric, they have been effective users of the Internet, not just to transmit information about their cause, but also to craft coalitions of international support. Labor leaders in Mexican *maquiladora* plants now routinely conduct e-mail campaigns against employers and government agencies.[29]

The Internet has begun to empower still-invisible minorities. One such group in most countries, including advanced democracies, is the gay and lesbian community. The Internet is more likely to benefit these disenfranchised groups than the already enfranchised. It is not surprising, therefore, that gay and lesbian sites have boomed in Latin America in the last few years, allowing Latin American gays to jump quickly from anonymity to connectivity. Gay activists in Argentina recently used the Internet to mount a successful letter-writing campaign that pressured a local governor into providing HIV medication to an imprisoned lesbian.[30] The Internet helps undermine the desire of marginalized groups to hide, and offers them a tool for asserting their rights.[31]

Market Reforms and Connectivity

Despite these inroads, connectivity in Latin America remains in its infancy. Access to the Internet covers less than 3 percent of the population in most Latin American countries (see table 2). The most connected country is Chile, and even there, only 4.2 percent of the population uses the Internet, compared to 40.7 percent in the United States and 36.3 percent in Canada. The telecommunications revolution might have begun in Latin America, but it is nowhere near its full potential. Latin America remains today largely an unconnected society.

Will these numbers grow? Answering this question requires examining the factors that help propel the Internet. Four factors are crucial: (1) openness to technological investments and innovation; (2) the rise of independent state regulatory agencies that promote competition among service providers; (3) the rise of computer literacy; and (4) the rise in the purchasing power of citizens.

To what extent do market reforms in general, or even sectoral liberalization, contribute to Internet connectivity? Most Latin American governments have concluded that market reforms are sufficient. Argentina, Mexico, Peru, and Venezuela, for instance, have recently ended long periods of exclusivity in telecommunications, convinced that this is all that is needed to expand Internet connectivity.[32] Yet market reforms are not enough.

On the one hand, market reforms were necessary for Internet connectivity mostly because they made possible the first factor, openness to technological investments and innovation. Latin America in the 1990s stood out

Table 2. Latin America: Still the Unwired Society

	Main Telephone Lines (per 100 inhabitants)		Cellular Mobile Subscribers (0,000)		Cellular Mobile Subscribers (per 100 inhabitants)	Internet Users (0,000)		Internet Users (per 100 inhabitants)
	1986*	1999	1989*	1999	1999	1995	1999	(1999)
Aggressive Reformers								
Argentina	10.3	20.1	2.3	2,530	7.00	1.4	900	2.5
Bolivia	2.9	5.8	0.0	402	4.93	0.1	35	0.4
Chile	6.4	18.6	4.9	964	6.50	7.0	625	4.2
Mexico	9.6	11.2	8.5	7,262	7.83	0.4	2,453	2.6
Peru	3.1	6.7	0.0	990	3.92	0.4	389	1.5
Intermediate Reformers								
Brazil	8.8	14.9	0.0	15,032	8.95	1.2	4,000	2.4
Colombia	7.6	16.0	0.0	3,134	7.54	0.7	600	1.6
Shallow Reformers								
Cuba	5.3	3.9	0.0	5	0.05	0.0	60	0.5
Ecuador	3.6	9.1	0.0	383	3.09	0.4	20	0.2
Paraguay	2.4	5.5	0.0	436	8.13	NA	20	0.4
Venezuela	8.9	10.9	3.7	3,400	14.34	0.5	400	1.7

Source: International Telecommunication Union, "Americas Telecommunication Indicators 2000" (Geneva: ITU, 2000).
* Department of Economic and Social Affairs Statistics Division. Statistical Yearbook, various issues (United Nations, 1992). This source is based on figures from the International Telecommunication Union.

as the region in the world that pursued market reforms most aggressively. It is not surprising that this is also the region that has experienced the fastest growth of Internet hosts in the last few years (see table 1). These reforms made possible the liberalization of capital markets, which guaranteed the necessary foreign investments to embark on the telecommunications revolution. Even countries that did not liberalize their economies fully, such as Venezuela, privatized their telephone companies nonetheless. The Americas contain the highest percentage of countries to have privatized telecommunication services, which made possible an enormous influx of investment and technology into the sector.

On the other hand, the role of markets in furthering the other three factors for connectivity has been more ambiguous, at times even negative. Market reforms in Latin America were often more concerned with changing the structure of ownership (privatization) than diversifying the structure of the market (injecting competition).[33] Telecommunication services, especially international connections, were often privatized under monopoly agreements, or with huge barriers to entry for new competitors. As of 1999 no more than one-third of Latin American countries allowed competition in basic phone services.[34] This permitted telecoms to charge per-minute access rates (as opposed to flat rates, as in the United States), thus discouraging Internet use. In Mexico, the government granted the privatized Telmex a monopoly over fixed and nonfixed lines, created legal barriers to entry, and restricted foreign control.[35] In Brazil, the government imposed restrictions on high-tech imports, including strict procurement policies and requirements that telecom carriers give preference to domestic companies for procurement of equipment.[36]

In Latin America as a whole, regulatory agencies that ensure fair competitive practices were left weak. After privatizing Telmex in 1990, Mexico waited six years to establish a regulatory agency (Cofetel).[37] And even then, Cofetel was designed without any real enforcement authority. Telmex thus has disproportionate clout with regard to Cofetel.[38] Consequently, it has been difficult to inject competition in Mexico. In August 2000, with pressure from the United States, local telecom rivals began to pressure Cofetel to take action against Telmex, accusing the firm of undermining competition by setting high interconnection costs. Each time Cofetel has ruled against Telmex, Telmex has taken legal action to resist. In January 2001 Telmex agreed to reduce rates, but interconnection fees remained five times higher than the cost price, displeasing Telmex's rivals.[39] In February 2002 the United States took the fight against Telmex to the World Trade Organization, a blunt recognition of the powerlessness of Cofetel. The persistence of some market concentration and weak regulatory capacity has placed brakes on the Internet revolution.

The role of market reforms with regard to the third factor, computer literacy, has also been ambiguous. This issue is linked to the question of education, which is in a sorry state throughout Latin America.[40] On the one hand, market reforms have softened Latin America's educational deficit by liberating new resources. On the other hand, real improvements in education depend less on resources than on maximizing the efficiency of the institutions that deliver education services. This is contingent on bureaucratic and legal reforms: restructuring the budget so that relatively more money goes into primary and secondary education; granting greater autonomy to schools; improving evaluation of performance of teachers and students; providing incentives for teachers to sharpen skills.[41] Market reformers have not been too concerned with these issues.[42] Thus, the impact of market reforms on education has been mild—neither enormously helpful nor enormously hurtful.

The effect of market reforms on the fourth factor, purchasing power, is controversial.[43] Essentially, this is a question about poverty rates, perhaps the most serious structural ceiling to connectivity. As long as Latin America exhibits stratospheric indices of poverty, the Internet revolution will remain unaffordable to most Latin Americans. In Brazil, for instance, it is estimated that only 20 percent of the population can afford Internet access (not including the cost of a personal computer). Among Argentina's upper class (the top quintile of the population), 74 percent of citizens own a computer and 56 percent use the Internet; in the low- and middle-income groups (the bottom half of the population), the figures drop to 6 percent and 4 percent, respectively.

Some scholars contend that market reforms aggravate poverty. The restructuring of the public sector, they argue, depresses the capacity of local economies to create sufficient employment, generating more losers than winners. Fiscal discipline and excessive concern with maintaining a favorable business climate constrain the state from raising the necessary taxes to deploy adequate relief and retooling for losers. Others argue that the reforms are helpful because they stopped the steep increase in inequality and poverty of the 1980s. Still others argue that the impact of reforms on poverty varies across countries (with Chile actually registering improvements) or across sectors (with some sectors experiencing improvements in wages and employment).[44] At best, the most that the defenders of reform can say about the impact of market reforms on poverty is that it has been irrelevant, too confined, or only modestly beneficial.

In short, market reforms have both facilitated and hindered the Internet revolution. For this reason, it would be naive to conclude that more market liberalization is enough for expanding Internet connectivity.

Internet Connectivity and Democratic Theory

The evolution of the Internet in Latin America offers several insights for the literature on the rise of democratic institutions. Internet connectivity can be construed as a right that democratic regimes provide to citizens, equivalent to other rights, such as the right to vote or the right to life, education, health, or happiness. Intermediate regimes guarantee these rights in their constitutions, but not always in fact. Latin American citizens have gained more access to the Internet than citizens elsewhere in the developing world. In some ways, this outcome conforms to existing models of democratization; in other respects, it defies them.

The evolution of the Internet in Latin America thus far confirms two standard accounts of the origins of democratic institutions. The first is the argument that democratization is somehow related to international pressures and some domestic economic crisis or dire economic condition, which combine to pressure states to liberalize.[45] Insofar as states have embarked on market reforms as a result of international pressures as well as dire domestic circumstances, one could assert that Internet connectivity has been the result—albeit indirectly— of these democracy-inducing pressures.

The second is the "elites-first" nature of most democratization processes. Scholars agree that the extension of democratic rights occurs in sequence. The most elite sectors obtain most rights first, followed by lesser groups, sometimes a couple of centuries later.[46] Likewise, the first beneficiaries of the Internet revolution in Latin America have been elite sectors: the upper- and middle-income groups, business leaders and their firms, the intelligentsia, students at private universities, etc. Two overlapping societal groups remain conspicuously un-wired: low-income groups (the bulk of the population) and low-education groups (students in public schools).

It is here that the first major difference with standard models of democratization surfaces. Elite groups have not been the only first beneficiaries of the Internet. Representative organizations of civil society (political parties, lobbying groups, university sectors, nonprofit organizations, advocacy groups, and watchdog groups) were early Internet users. The wiring of these organizations occurred before that of their own constituents, and even of some elites. The societal map of Internet access is therefore characterized by twin peaks: one occupied by elites, the other, by organizations of civil society (see figure 1). This twin-peak character is one of the most distinctive features of the Internet revolution thus far.

Another difference with standard models of democratization has to do with the extent to which this process has been the product of "contentious collective action," to borrow Sidney Tarrow's phrase.[47] Most accounts of the origin of democratic institutions are predicated on the notion of struggle. Rights-starved sectors of society wrestle against a resistant state and its allies. States, for the most part, repress these claims, unless rights-demanding groups achieve sufficient political force—or "bargaining power," to borrow from Charles Tilly.

This "tug of war" view of the origin of democratic rights captures some, but not all, elements of the politics of Internet connectivity. It captures the process of infusing competition in the telecommunication sector in the early 1990s: privatized telecom firms resisted societal demands for more competitive long-distance rates. But it does not capture the main reason that connectivity has reached a ceiling. It is simply not the case that Internet expansion is constrained because the state and the right-holding sectors (the already-wired groups) are intrinsically opposed to it. The barrier to further expansion is not conflict of interest.

Coordination as a Political Barrier to Connectivity

The most important political barrier hindering Internet expansion to these sectors, in addition to the socioeconomic structural barrier discussed previously, is a coordination dilemma.[48] To understand this, consider the

Figure 1. The "Twin Peaks" of Internet Access

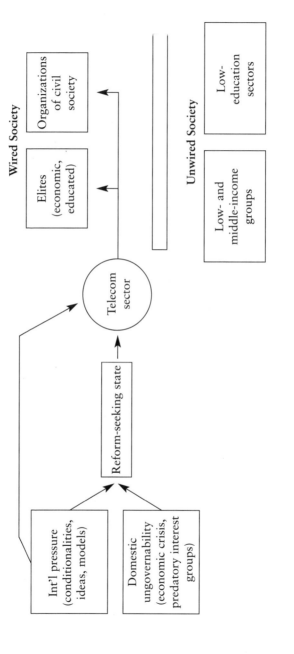

challenge of wiring public schools in any country, which is an efficient way to enlarge access to the Internet for low-income groups. The private sector should naturally welcome such an expansion. Yet on its own, the private sector will not furnish the necessary investment. If the private sector is to make a profit from such a large project, the various entities within the private sector must act in unison. Computer manufacturers must agree to provide computers at affordable prices: telecoms and Internet service providers must offer discounted rates; and the financial sector needs to provide subsidized loans. Each entity requires assurances that the others will fulfill their part. On its own, the private sector is unlikely to solve this problem. What is needed is a coordinating agent—that is, an authority that can offer guarantees that each of these steps will take place, an information broker of sorts.

The state is ideally situated to play this coordinating role. Latin America offers examples of two possible solutions. In mid-2000 the Argentine government launched a computer literacy campaign *(campaña de alfabetización informática),* whereby the government promised to wire all schools. This guaranteed economies of scale to the private sector. Instantly, interest on the part of the private sector grew, allowing the state to negotiate private-sector commitments: manufacturers agreed to provide computers at a discount, the Banco de la Nación agreed to provide credit and easy financing terms to the new buyers, and Internet providers agreed to provide free connections.[49] By ensuring economies of scale and coordinating commitments among different entities of the private sector, the Argentine state could very well have designed an effective model for overcoming political obstacles to Internet expansion. Unfortunately, Argentina's 2001–2002 economic crisis paralyzed this effort. Nonetheless, this initiative is a good model of state-led coordination.

A second policy option is for the state to rely on local communities and nongovernmental organizations (NGOs), brokering agreements between them and the private sector. As already noted, the first beneficiaries of Internet connectivity have been organizations of civil society, especially NGOs. That these civil-society sectors are already wired—and deeply interested in further Internet expansion—provides an excellent opportunity for states. In partnership with the state (and business groups), NGOs could take the lead in such projects as developing computer training programs for teachers, students, and community leaders. Training teachers is indispensable since one of the biggest obstacles to Internet use in schools is that teachers themselves lack computer literacy, and thus do not become promoters of computer use. Expanding Internet connectivity is a perfect arena for building pro-development coalitions among the state, NGOs, business firms, and multilaterals.[50]

The "Infoplaza" Project launched in Panama in 1999–2000 is a good example.[51] The Infoplazas are a series of cabins located throughout the country, mostly in rural and poor areas, equipped with ten to twenty multimedia computers (with Web tools, multiple servers, e-mail, and other communication tools), back-up equipment, air conditioning, and other amenities. The project began when the government became concerned over the lack of computer access in schools in low-income zones and rural areas. It entrusted the National Bureau of Science, Technology, and Innovation (SENACYT) to form a commission made up of public- and private-sector representatives, as well as academics. After obtaining financing from a multilateral (the Inter-American Development Bank), the commission began to visit potential target areas and to interview families, local churches, local libraries, neighborhood assemblies, health clinics, and local NGOs, asking them, "What exactly would you like, and how much would you be willing to pay?" Those communities that indicated strong commitment were encouraged to form a local NGO, if none existed. The commission then contacted telecom operators, local electricity providers, computer providers, and banks to ensure the necessary investments.[52] The government would formalize the legal contract between the local NGO, the providers, and the lenders, committing all parties to create the Infoplazas. Microsoft agreed to provide software, Samsung provided hardware, a local telecom provided access, and domestic and foreign lenders provided financing. CISCO provided training to local NGOs, which would then develop their own local training programs.

The cost of each Infoplaza ranges from $6,000 to $22,000, not an exorbitant amount. But without the coordinating role of the state, which brokered the involvement of local NGOs, international and local lenders, and the private telecom sector, this form of wiring would not have materialized. The state is intervening, not in the old-fashioned way of shouldering the investments, but as a coordinating agent that galvanizes nonstate actors to make investments. As of February 2002, more than thirty Infoplazas operated in Panama, many of them in rural areas.[53]

Different States, Different Internet Incentives

The key question then is what incentives do states have to engage in this coordinating role? Herein lies the problem. Unlike the private sector, which has a strong desire to see Internet expansion, the state might not perceive any immediate tangible gains. It is not that the state is necessarily opposed to Internet expansion, but rather, that its preference is less intense than that of the private sector. The only serious incentive that the state has to expand the Internet is often international pressure. Insofar as states come to realize that connectivity is a crucial component of international competitiveness, they might feel pressed to expand connectivity. But even this pressure could be unreliable: the promise of international competitiveness via Internet development is too vague and long-term, and thus easy for states to forego. It is important, therefore, to assess whether there are any other incentives that might motivate states to engage in expanding the Internet.

Not all states are similar, and some differences are pivotal in determining state interest in promoting the Internet. One crucial difference is whether states are authoritarian or democratic. Each has different motivations for (and reservations about) expanding the Internet.

Authoritarian states have two substantial reasons for being interested in the Internet. First, they have an intense desire to engage in surveillance of dissidents, which the Internet allows them to do. Second, many authoritarian states try to compensate for the lack of domestic legitimacy by boosting their international standing. These states might feel more need to develop the Internet as a way to achieve a more "modern" reputation abroad. By modernizing their economy, they hope to lure foreign investors and thus gain external respectability. Again, economic openness increases government interest in developing the Internet because of the realization that in a globalized world, being behind in Internet development hinders competitiveness.

Yet there is an important reason that authoritarian states prefer not to expand the Internet: their fear of the democratizing potential of the Internet. Market-authoritarian regimes, such as China, Saudi Arabia, and Singapore, confront a dilemma: the market compels them to develop a technology that in the end allows their citizens to escape authoritarian controls.[54]

Thus, authoritarian regimes hold two strong and opposite preferences with regard to the Internet: they want it, but they fear it. The more internationally minded the authoritarian regime is, the more it will want to expand the Internet, but this desire will always be tempered by a very strong concern to circumscribe Internet usage domestically.

In democratic states these two preferences—to want it and to fear it—tend to be weaker. Because democracies have less to worry about regarding issues of domestic legitimacy, they might feel less pressed than authoritarian states to court international supporters and monitor dissidents, and hence might be less inclined to promote the Internet. But democracies do not share the fear of empowering civil society that paralyzes authoritarian regimes. On their own, therefore, democratic governments in developing countries might not necessarily develop the desire to promote the Internet, but they will not be actively opposed to it. This means that they can be compelled to go in that direction far more easily than authoritarian governments, but only if they experience the right pressures from nonstate actors. Precisely because democratic states, by definition, are more porous and open to societal pressure, nonstate actors have a higher chance of persuading them to become involved in Internet development. Internet expansion in democratic contexts is more likely to go forward when states, NGOs, business groups, and multilaterals join forces.

Several generalizations can now be made about the extent to which the Internet is likely to expand in developing countries. Table 3 classifies states according to the three politico-economic factors that matter most for Internet expansion: whether states are democratic or authoritarian, whether or not they are market-oriented, and whether they govern societies with high or low levels of poverty. Table 3 also summarizes the crucial factors that motivate or constrain each type of state with regard to engaging in Internet promotion activities: concern with courting international actors, desire to engage in surveillance, susceptibility to pressure from external forces (civil society and business groups), and socioeconomic barriers. The following propositions emerge:

Table 3. Types of States and Factors Contributing to Internet Expansion

Type of State	Incentives to Promote the Internet — Export promotion and attract FDI	Incentives to Promote the Internet — Surveillance/monitoring	Disincentives to Promote the Internet; Fear of Empowering Citizens	Role of State-Society Factors — Susceptibility to demands from societal actors	Role of State-Society Factors — Socio-economic barriers	Outcome: Internet Expansion (example, number of users per 10,000 inhabitants in 2000)
Authoritarian						
Non-market-oriented	low	high	high	low		**Nil** Myanmar: 0.21 Equatorial Guinea: 11.2 Azerbaijan: 15.5
Semi-market-oriented	medium	high	high	low		**Medium-low** Cuba: 53.6
Market-oriented	high	high	high	low		**Medium** China: 173.7 Oman: 354.6
Market-oriented democracy						
Low poverty	high	medium	low	high	low	**High** South Korea: 4025.4
Medium poverty	high	medium	low	high	medium	**Medium-high** Chile: 1155.31
High poverty	high	medium	low	high	high	**Medium** Brazil: 293.2
Non-market-oriented democracy						
High poverty	low	low	low	low	high	**Medium-low** Paraguay: 37.32
High poverty, middle-income	low	low	low	medium	high	Venezuela: 393.1

1. Highly repressive, inward-oriented regimes are the least likely to promote the Internet (Myanmar, Equatorial Guinea, Azerbaijan).

2. Market-oriented authoritarian states exhibit a stronger desire to develop the Internet (Oman, China). Yet this preference is still tempered by a fear of empowering civil society. Thus, market-oriented authoritarian states will develop the Internet further than non–market-oriented authoritarian states (compare China and Oman with Myanmar, Equatorial Guinea, and Azerbaijan), but never to an impressive degree (compare China and Oman with South Korea).

3. Democratic states might not necessarily feel the urgent pressure to develop the Internet that motivates market-oriented authoritarian regimes, yet they are much more easily persuaded to engage in Internet expansion policies if the right coalition of nonstate pressures materializes (NGOs, business groups, international donors).

4. Among democracies, market-oriented states are more likely to promote the Internet than less market-oriented democracies (South Korea vs. Venezuela). They care about international investment and they generate the necessary market forces to permit Internet expansion.

5. The efforts of market-oriented democracies will go only as far as socioeconomic conditions allow. The higher the levels of poverty, the higher the barriers for Internet expansion (compare South Korea, Brazil, Chile, and Venezuela), making it all the more imperative for states, NGOs, and business groups to coordinate their actions.

Conclusion

Internet connectivity in developing countries ought be seen as both an effect and a cause of democratization. Developing countries that are fledgling market-oriented democracies provide the perfect site for the Internet to make a political difference. There the Internet stands a higher chance of expanding, and there it can have a more democratic impact, empowering citizens to deal with the imperfections typical of these regimes.

The expansion of the Internet in Latin America, although incipient, already provides the opportunity to assess standard theories about the origins of democratic rights. Internet connectivity, like many previously obtained democratic rights, has had a complex relationship with market forces. Access to the Internet is hard to imagine in the absence of liberalized economies. Yet, there remain two fundamental barriers to Internet connectivity—and, by extension, economic competitiveness—in developing countries. One is structural and harder to solve in the short-term: low levels of schooling and high levels of poverty. The second barrier is strategic: coordinating difficulties among the potential investors.

In the case of Internet expansion, the coordination dilemma is serious. The private sector has an intense desire to develop the Internet, but it lacks the capacity to coordinate expansion activities. The state has a superb capacity to act as coordinating agent, yet it has a milder or even conflicted desire to make such investments. This asymmetry in the intensity of preferences and coordinating capacities between the two leading suppliers of connectivity—the state and the market—sets brakes on the economic competitiveness of developing countries. It should be clear, however, that market reforms are not enough and that authoritarian regimes are not necessarily suited to solve this dilemma. What is necessary is the combination of a market-oriented *and* a democratic state. This type of state is the most amenable to the kind of state–civil society partnerships necessary for promoting the Internet. Until this lesson is well understood, the prospects of Internet expansion will be in question.

Notes

I am enormously grateful to the Woodrow Wilson International Center for Scholars, Washington, D.C., for supporting this research, and to Taylor Boas, Margaret Crahan, Larry Diamond, Jorge I. Domínguez, Kent Hughes, Margaret Keck, Peter Lewis, James McGuire, Martha Merritt, Leslie Simon, Frank Westhoff, and Beth Yarbrough for their invaluable comments. I am also indebted to Patricia del Grosso for her resourcefulness as my research assistant.

1. Don Tapscott and David Agnew, "Governance in the Digital Economy: The Importance of Human Development," *Finance and Development* 36 (1999): 44.

2. See chapters in Barry N. Hague and Brian D. Loader, eds., *Digital Democracy: Discourse and Decision Making in the Information Age* (New York: Routledge, 1999).

3. Bruce Bimber, "The Internet and Political Transformation: Populism, Community, and Accelerated Pluralism," *Polity* 31, no. 1 (1998): 133–160.

4. Larry Diamond, "Is the Third Wave Over?" *Journal of Democracy* 7, no. 3 (1996): 20–37.

5. Seymour Martin Lipset, *Political Man: The Social Bases of Politics* (Garden City, N.Y.: Doubleday, 1960).

6. Aaron Pressman, "Lessons for Campaign 2004," *Industry Standard*, 13 November 2000.

7. The evidence that the Internet is reducing the appetite for information is inconclusive. It is true that "news consumption" is not the favorite pastime of Internet users, trailing behind other uses, such as updates on stocks and sports, and weather and movie information. However, news consumption has grown dramatically in recent years. In addition, there is evidence that the Internet serves as a mechanism for deepening information: 41 percent of those who go online say they turn to the Internet "to get more information" on stories first seen in the traditional media. See Pew Research Center, "Online Newcomers More Middle-Brow, Less Work-Oriented: The Internet News Audience Goes Ordinary" (1998), at <http://www.people-press.org/tech98sum.htm>. A survey in the United States showed that one in three Americans in 2000 went online for news at least once a week, compared to one in five in 1998. Internet news is attracting many younger people who have only a marginal interest in the news. Thus, rather than fueling cynicism toward politics, the Internet might actually be doing the opposite: encouraging the otherwise disengaged public to become more interested in current events. See Pew Research Center, "Internet Sapping Broadcast News Audience" (2000), at <http://www.people-press.org/media00rpt.htm>.

8. Bimber, "Internet and Political Transformation."

9. Rachel Gibson, "Elections Online: Assessing Internet Voting in Light of the Arizona Democratic Primary," *Political Science Quarterly* 116, no. 4 (winter 2001–2002): 561–584.

10. Jessica T. Mathews, "The Information Revolution," *Foreign Policy* 119 (summer 2000): 63–69.

11. Jean K. Chalaby, "New Media, New Freedoms, New Threats," *Gazette* 62, no. 1 (2000): 19–29.

12. The Gore/Nader vote-swapping plan consisted of an effort by individual Gore Democrats in easy Republican states such as Texas to pair with individual Nader supporters in swing states such as Michigan. Nader supporters in swing states would vote for Gore in exchange for a Gore supporter in an easy Republican state to vote for Nader. That way, Nader could get the 5 percent of the popular vote he needed to secure federal matching funds for

the Green Party in 2004 without tipping swing states to George W. Bush and costing Gore the electoral votes he needed to win.

13. Richard K. Moore, "Democracy and Cyberspace," in *Digital Democracy,* ed. Hague and Loader.

14. Secret Internet messages, known as steganography, are one of the most insidious ways of using the Internet for criminal purposes. See Adam Cohen, "When Terror Hides Online," *Time*, 12 November 2001, 65.

15. See Norman Nie and Lutz Erbring, "Internet and Society: A Preliminary Report" (Stanford, Calif.: Stanford Institute for the Quantitative Study of Society, February 2000), at <www.stanford.edu/group/siqss>.

16. On how the new information-based technologies might corrupt democracy, see Timothy W. Luke, "Digital Beings and Virtual Times: The Politics of Cybersubjectivity," *Theory and Event* 1 (1997): 1; and Benjamin R. Barber, "Three Scenarios for the Future of Technology and Strong Democracy," *Political Science Quarterly* 113, no. 4 (1998–1999): 573–589.

17. For a discussion of "control" issues, see Barry N. Hague and Brian D. Loader, "Digital Democracy: An Introduction," in *Digital Democracy,* ed. Hague and Loader. For a discussion of "usage" issues, see John Arquilla, David Ronfeldt, and Michele Zanini, "Information-Age Terrorism," *Current History* (April 2000): 179–185; Chalaby, "New Media, New Freedoms, New Threats."

18. Adrian Karatnycky, "A Century of Progress: The 1999 Freedom House Survey," *Journal of Democracy* 11, no. 1 (January 2000): 187–200.

19. Inter-American Development Bank, *Development beyond Economics: Economic and Social Progress in Latin America* (Washington, D.C.: Inter-American Development Bank, 2000), 23–26, 184.

20. International Telecommunication Union, "Americas Telecommunication Indicators 2000" (April 2000).

21. As impressive as the Internet revolution might be, the real information revolution will occur once the Internet becomes fully wireless, potentially ending a major barrier to connectivity—geographically constrained wires. This has been called "the conquest of location." See John Micklethwait and Adrian Wool-

dridge, *A Future Perfect : The Challenge and Hidden Promise of Globalization* (New York: Times Books, 2000), 29–45.

22. International Telecommunication Union, "Americas Telecommunication Indicators 2000."

23. For a more skeptical, but nonetheless positive view on the democratizing impact of the Internet in Latin America, see Ricardo Gómez, "The Hall of the Mirrors: The Internet in Latin America," *Current History* 99, no. 634 (May 2000): 72–77.

24. Market Analysis Brazil, "Feedback: A Quarterly Summary of Key Findings from Our Opinion and Market Research" (summer 2001), at <www.portadigital.com.br/~market/news43>.

25. In the Philippines, another intermediate democracy, mobile telephones helped topple the corrupt president Joseph Estrada. Organizers of a protest against the president sent the message "Full mblsn tday Edsa," translated as "full mobilization today at Edsa shrine in Manila," to every mobile user they knew. They were able to organize a march with hundreds of thousands of protesters. See "A Survey of Technology and Development," *The Economist,* 10 November 2001, 16.

26. Omaira Sayago, "El Nacional.com registra 2 millones de páginas vistas por días," *El Nacional* (Caracas), 10 January 2002.

27. *Clarín* (Buenos Aires), 26 April 2002.

28. *La Nación* (Buenos Aires), 11 March 2002.

29. Pete Engardio, "Activists without Borders," *Business Week,* 4 October 1999, 144–150.

30. Elizabeth Love, "Community Center: Latin America's Gay and Lesbian Population Emerges from the Cyber Closet," *Latin-Trade* (December 2000).

31. The effects of the Internet on gay communities are also visible outside Latin America. In Zimbabwe, for instance, since at least 1996, gays have responded to President Mugabe's attacks by jumping on the Internet and organizing international protests against him. *The Economist*, 6 January 1996, 70.

32. A good example of this attitude is the fact that Mexican president Vicente Fox's finance minister Francisco Gil Díaz was the president of the country's largest Internet service provider (AVANTEL), who led the fight in the late 1990s against Telmex's

monopoly. Gil Díaz also obtained his Ph.D. from the University of Chicago, where he studied under Milton Friedman.

33. On why the reforms produce liberalized and nonliberalized sectors, see Javier Corrales, "Market Reforms in Latin America: Why They Were Done, Why They Were Not So Market Oriented," in *Constructing Democratic Governance*, ed. Jorge I. Domínguez and Michael Shifter, 2d ed. (Baltimore, MD: Johns Hopkins University Press, forthcoming).

34. See M.Victoria Murillo, "Inventing Markets: Public Utility Privatization in Argentina, Chile, and Mexico," Paper presented at the APSA Congress, September 2001.

35. U.S. Department of Commerce, "ExportIT Latin America" (Washington, D.C.: International Trade Administration, U.S. Department of Commerce, June 2000).

36. It is not coincidental that telephone service hardly increased during this period. Main telephone lines per 100 inhabitants in 1996 were exactly at the same level as in 1986 (around 9.6). International Telecommunications Union, "Americas Telecommunication Indicators 2000."

37. *The Economist*, "After the Revolution: A Survey of Mexico," 28 October 2000, 6.

38. "Telecom Battle Goes Back to WTO," *Latin America Monitor* 19, no. 3 (March 2002): 8.

39. Inter-American Development Bank, *Development beyond Economics;* Jeffrey M. Puryear, "Education in Latin America: Problems and Challenges," Occasional Paper Series No. 7 (Washington, D.C.: PREAL/Inter-American Dialogue, May 1997); Juan Carlos Navarro, Martín Carnoy, Claudio de Moura Castro, "Education Reform in Latin America and the Caribbean" (Washington, D.C.: Inter-American Development Bank, 1998).

40. William D. Savedoff, "Social Services Viewed through New Lenses," in *Organization Matters: Agency Problems in Health and Education in Latin America* (Washington, D.C.: Inter-American Development Bank, 1998); Françoise Delannoy, "Reformas en Gestión Educacional," Latin America and the Caribbean, Human Development Department Paper Series No. 21 (Washington, D.C.: World Bank, 1998); Joan M. Nelson, *Reforming*

Health and Education: The World Bank, the IDB, and Complex Institutional Change (Washington, D.C.: Overseas Development Council, 1999).

41. For a more detailed analysis, see Martin Carnoy, "Structural Adjustment and the Changing Face of Education," *International Labour Review* 135, no. 6 (1995): 653–673.

42. U.S. Department of Commerce, "ExportIT Latin America."

43. See, for instance, Victor Bulmer-Thomas, ed., *The New Economic Model in Latin America and Its Impact on Income Distribution and Poverty* (London: Macmillan, 1996); Albert Berry, ed., *Poverty, Economic Reform, and Income Distribution in Latin America* (Boulder, Colo.: Lynn Rienner Publishers, 1998); Oscar Altimir, "Inequality, Employment, and Poverty in Latin America: An Overview,"in *Poverty and Inequality in Latin America: Issues and New Challenges*, ed. Víctor E. Tokman and Guillermo O'Donnell (Notre Dame, Ind.: Notre Dame University Press, 1998); Philip Oxhorn and Graciela Ducatenzeiler, "The Problematic Relationship between Economic and Political Liberalization: Some Theoretical Considerations," in *Markets and Democracy in Latin America: Conflict or Convergence?* ed. Philip Oxhorn and Pamela K. Starr (Boulder, Colo.: Lynne Rienner Publishers, 1999); Robert N. Gwynne and Cristóbal Kay, "Views from the Periphery: Futures of Neoliberalism in Latin America," *Third World Quarterly* 21, no. 1 (2000): 141–156.

44. Part of the reason for these disagreements is that when researchers observe certain trends in poverty indices—improvements or deterioration—they find it difficult to isolate the exact cause (the overall reforms, certain components of the reforms, certain omissions from the reforms, lingering effects from the 1980s, responses to poststabilization consumer booms, and so forth). For a review of these controversies, see John Sheahan, "Effects of Changing Economic Strategies on Inequality," paper presented at the annual meeting of the New England Council of Latin American Studies, Yale University, New Haven, Conn., 16 October 1999; Roberto Patricio Korzeniewicz, "The Deepening Differentiation of State, Enterprises, and Households in Latin America," in *Politics, Social Change and Economic Restructuring in Latin America*, ed. William C. Smith and Roberto Patricio Korze-

niewicz (Miami: University of Miami, North-South Center Press, 1997); Roberto Patricio Korzeniewicz and William C. Smith, "Growth, Poverty, and Inequality in Latin America: Searching for the High Road to Globalization," *Latin American Research Review* 35, no. 3 (2000):7–56; Barbara Stallings and Wilson Peres, *Growth, Employment, and Equity: The Impact of Economic Reforms in Latin America and the Caribbean* (Washington, D.C.: Brookings Institution, 2000).

45. Lawrence Whitehead, ed., *The International Dimensions of Democratization: Europe and the Americas*, expanded ed. (New York: Oxford University Press, 2001); Stephan Haggard and Robert R. Kaufman, *The Political Economy of Democratic Transitions* (Princeton, N.J.: Princeton University Press, 1995).

46. Charles Tilly, *Coercion, Capital, and European States, A.D. 990–1990* (Cambridge, Mass.: B. Blackwell, 1990).

47. Sidney G. Tarrow, *Power in Movement: Social Movements and Contentious Politics,* Cambridge Studies in Comparative Politics (Cambridge: Cambridge University Press, 1994).

48. For a discussion of the coordination dilemma as a barrier to economic development in general, and export promotion in particular, see Joseph Stiglitz, "Some Lessons from the East Asian Miracle," *World Bank Research Observer* 2 (August 1996): 151–177.

49. *Clarín* (Buenos Aires), 18 July 2000.

50. On the potential benefits for development of partnerships among states, NGOs, and multilaterals, see Korzeniewicz and Smith, "Poverty, Inequality, and Growth in Latin America."

51. For a fuller description of this initiative, see Azael Barrera, "Empowering the Rural and Poor Suburban Communities in Central America: The Infoplazas Program of Panama," paper presented at the International Seminar on Integrating Modern and Traditional Information and Communication Technologies for Development, Mawatura, Sri Lanka, 22–27 January 2001, available online at <www.unesco.org/public_domain/kothmale_docs/panam.rtf>.

52. Not all actors joined this initiative eagerly. The British telecommunications firm Cable and Wireless, which owns the local telephone company in monopoly form until 2003, was re-

luctant to offer the necessary discounts. The government finally managed to convince the firm to subsidize the program by as much as 70 percent, in some cases. See Varrera, "Empowering the Rural and Poor Suburban Communities in Central America," 6.

53. "Internet en Panamá," *CNN en Español*, Latin America cable edition, 25 February 2002.

54. See Leslie D. Simon, "The Net: Power and Policy in the 21st Century" (Washington, D.C.: Woodrow Wilson Center, 2000). For a good review of China's "conflicting desires" over Internet development, see Shanthi Kalathil, "China's Dot-Communism," *Foreign Policy* (January–February 2001): 74–75.

CHAPTER 3

 Congress and the Internet:
Democracy's
Uncertain Link

Donald R. Wolfensberger

By September 2001 the U.S. Congress, arguably the
world's most important and visible democratic institution, had begun to test the uses of the Internet and advanced information technology in its work. It had made
progress in some areas and faltered in others, but overall Congress had done a better job in legislating new
rules for the Internet than it had in using the Internet
itself. Then came the events of September 11 and the
anthrax episodes that followed. Suddenly, the Internet
began to play a more central role in Congress's primary
democratic functions of legislating and communicating
with constituents. This sudden acceleration in the use of
advanced information technology has powerful implications for how democratic institutions will be directly affected by the digital revolution.

Earlier in 2001, at a Woodrow Wilson Center Roundtable, a senior congressional staff member had presciently
stated that the stark choice confronting Congress over the

Internet and advanced information technology was to "adapt or die."[1] Little could the staffer have known then just how literal his admonition would turn out to be only ten months later. On October 15, 2001, a little over a month after terrorists attacked the World Trade Center and the Pentagon, the very walls of Congress were penetrated by a different type of terrorism from an anthrax-laced envelope addressed to Senate Majority Leader Tom Daschle (D-S.D.). The spores released from that envelope threatened the lives of hundreds of congressional staffers and the senators for whom they worked in the Hart Senate Office Building.

As a precautionary measure, all House and Senate office buildings were shut down on October 18. The anthrax attack nearly brought the wheels of our representative democracy to a halt. The House adjourned on October 17, while the Senate worked on for another day in the Capitol Building. Not only were regular mail deliveries to House and Senate offices halted, but the sudden closure of congressional office buildings temporarily severed vital phone and computer links between most members and their constituents.

Congress was thus forced to deal with two crises simultaneously: how to legislatively address the national problems arising from the September 11 attacks and how to continue to function as a national legislature in a state of dislocation. While the General Accounting Office graciously abandoned two floors of its own building near Capitol Hill for members and staff, other members found colleagues with Capitol hideaway offices they were willing to share, worked out of their homes, or returned to their congressional district offices. Most important, laptop computers were bought for the members and staff to use (two per House office), wherever they might be working. Under the literal threat of death, Congress was forced to adapt by relying on information-age technologies in order to survive and function as a legislative body.

Picking BlackBerries

Members were kept up to date by their leadership on floor scheduling, caucus meetings, health alerts, and building closure developments via computer, cell phone, pager, and Palm Pilot. In the wake of the anthrax incident, the House Administration Committee authorized each member and senior staffers to purchase BlackBerries, a handheld, wireless e-mail device. Doug Heye, communications director for Rep. Richard Pombo (R-Calif.), observed of the BlackBerry that "on September 11, this technology was often the only way I could communicate," and "when the House buildings closed recently [following the anthrax attacks] I could not have done my job without it." [2]

One of the most gaping holes for members in this newly transfigured world was the complete cutoff of postal (so-called snail mail) deliveries. Rep. Jim Leach (R-Iowa) lamented, "People will begin to feel that their Congress is more distant from them, cut off, and Congress will miss a key balancing link in their legislative judgments." Rep. David Price (D-N.C.), a former political science professor at Duke, said the discontinuance of mail deliveries during a time of national crisis would only exacerbate the trauma since "people's contact is cut off at a time when they most need it." Sen. Kent Conrad (D-N.D.) underscored Leach's point about how the damage runs both ways: "If it goes on for a prolonged period, we're all going to feel cut off."[3]

While this crisis could have been the perfect opportunity for members of Congress to stay in touch with constituents by e-mail, the vast majority of House offices lost access to e-mail files when their buildings were shut down, because they had not bothered to establish secure IDs to access their files remotely, even though 50 percent of the offices had the capability to do so. Senators were similarly limited. Each office was given just two coded cards for remote-access purposes.

It is doubtful that even members and staff with access would have had the time to read their constituent e-mail from their cramped new quarters with only a limited number of computers and with staff already stretched thin. As was the case before the anthrax evacuation, most e-mail traffic was internal, among members and staff trying to address the important legislative business at hand under the most difficult circumstances. Only about 10 percent of members normally answer constituent e-mail messages by e-mail, preferring instead to use the more personal, member-signed snail mail for responses.

Because of the cyber-security firewalls, most congressional offices were not able to open their external e-mail messages until after their offices began to reopen on October 25, a week after the closure. One House member's office reported that whereas it ordinarily gets 500 e-mail messages a week, when it reopened, it found 2,000 messages waiting—a 400 percent increase.[4] Some members did try to keep abreast of their constituent e-mail messages while they were in temporary quarters. Several publicized their district office e-mail addresses, phone and fax numbers, and Web sites through local media. The Congress Online Project cites the example of Rep. Brad Carson (D-Okla.), who had shifted his correspondence management system to e-mail earlier in the year. When he and his staff were forced to evacuate the Cannon House Office Building, they were able to remotely access their files using a secure ID system that had been provided to them. Rep. Mike Pence (R-Ind.) was one of the unfortunate few members whose Longworth Building office was found to have anthrax traces in it. Because he had established a system that enabled his staff to remotely update his Web site, he was able to use it to contact constituents who had visited the office, urging them to be tested for the disease.[5]

Speaker Dennis Hastert (R-Ill.) and House Democratic Leader Richard Gephardt (D-Mo.) took the unprecedented action of publishing on their Web sites in late October a joint letter to the American people in which they explained how the anthrax attacks on the mail "have complicated the mail delivery process" in the House. "While we do not want to discourage you to contact your representatives," they went on, "alternatives may be more prudent for requests that require immediate attention." They called attention to the fact that most members have e-mail accounts and fax machines, and urged constituents to go to the members' Web sites for further information.[6]

It was not uncommon for members and committees to highlight on their Web sites what they were doing to assist in the war on terrorism (bills introduced, hearings held, bills reported, testimony of expert witnesses), and to provide useful health and safety information as a public service. One senator who stood out in this regard was Sen. Bill Frist (R-Tenn.), a physician, who used his Web page to provide information on anthrax and how to deal with it. At the top of Frist's home page were three boxes that visitors could access, on the following topics: "What to do if you receive an envelope or package suspected to contain anthrax or other biological agents"; "Submit your questions about bio-terrorism to a panel of experts"; and, "Anthrax and bio-terrorism information."[7] Frist's Web site was especially helpful and reassuring to other senators and their staff in the early stages of the anthrax incident, but it was also widely accessed by the public at large. Before the anthrax attack Frist's Web site had attracted about 4,000 hits a week, but during the last week in October it got more than 100,000 hits.[8]

Overall, the most notable use of new technologies during this crisis was the increased use of laptops and BlackBerries by members and staff as internal communication devices to keep the institution functioning. Under such difficult circumstances, it was a wonder that Congress was able to do as much as it did to operate and to keep the public informed. However, the anthrax scare and shutdown of congressional offices buildings were not typical examples of how well Congress is adapting to the information age and how it is using the new technologies to do a better job of lawmaking, oversight, and constituent service. Before the events of September 11, Congress had taken one step backward for every two steps forward in its approach to the Internet.

Two Scenarios

The "adapt or die" warning to Congress, mentioned earlier, is a distilled version of two information-age scenarios that twenty-seven House and Senate staff members participating in the Stennis Center's Congressional Staff Fellowship Program saw confronting Congress at the beginning of the new century.

In their final report, the staff members warned that if Congress does not take steps to deal with the twenty-first-century tempo, it could "risk the eventual death of deliberative or representative constitutional democracy" and its replacement by a political system "closer to direct democracy."[9] Their conclusions mirror other commentaries on how the Internet will affect American democracy generally, and the U.S. Congress in particular. The more optimistic view is that Internet use will lead to a more enlightened and engaged citizenry, a more communicative and informative Congress, and, consequently, the forging of closer ties between the people and their elected representatives. The gloomy view is that the Internet's development and popular use will overwhelm the ability of Congress to master this new medium and thereby lead to a more plebiscitary form of democracy, in which public opinion will replace deliberative decision-making in determining national policies.

The Stennis Staff Fellows listed likely consequences of each scenario, beginning with the pessimistic one:

- Congress could become dependent on technology and fall into the role of delegate. It could continue to aggregate interests rather than foster compromise, and deliberation could degenerate into cut-throat competition and confrontation between the parties.
- People could come to expect immediate answers from Congress as they become accustomed to immediate answers from information technology. Moreover, electronic communication could undermine personal contacts, so that Congress would be seen as less relevant and concerned.
- Congress could slip into a permanent campaign mode, more dependent on polling, focus groups, and campaign fundraising, and thus be unable to deliberate effectively.[10]

By contrast, the staff group projected the desirable scenario as follows:

- Congress could harness technology, act on it in a broad context, and use it as part of its leadership strategy to leverage policy making.
- Congress could spend most of its time governing in a "deliberative and constructively partisan" manner, and be "visionary, educational, [and] instrumental in creating a sense of national purpose."
- Congressional oversight could serve as a national educational and deliberative device by using information technology in innovative ways to engage the public.

- Institutional leadership could be directed to increasing public respect for Congress.[11]

The congressional staff veterans thought Congress could either remain relatively passive and allow itself to be overwhelmed by the information age revolution, or could become pro-active by using the new technologies to achieve its core functions of lawmaking, oversight, and constituent service, all without sacrificing the essential deliberative nature of the institution.

The Stennis Fellows' views were given a broader airing before a group of forty congressional staff and political scientists at a roundtable convened in January 2001 at the Woodrow Wilson Center.[12] It was clear that the totality of information-age technologies—not just the Internet—was affecting the Congress. This universe of technologies includes e-mail messages over the Internet, blast faxes, phone trees, talk radio, proliferating cable TV channels and twenty-four-hour news cycles, and instant polling—all of which amplify the volume of new voices on all manner of emerging issues.

The e-mail burden alone has proven especially frustrating for many congressional offices. One Stennis Fellow indicated that his office receives on average 3,000 e-mail messages a week from constituents. And yet, like many offices, it still attempts to answer them all with a regular signed letter from the representative.

A Congress Online Project survey in 2000 found that the volume of e-mail to congressional offices has risen from 20 million messages in 1998 to 48 million in 2000, and that it continues to grow on average by 1 million messages per month. Much of this mail is attributable

to grassroots lobbyists and e-businesses, which capitalize on the new technology to advance their cause. Unfortunately, the report concludes, "these advocacy
groups are encouraging the public to engage in e-mail
practices—like spamming congressional offices—that
result in unmanageable demands on Congress."[13]

The congressional staff group concluded that even
though the ability of new technologies to empower individuals and new virtual communities is still in its forma-
tive stages, it is already affecting every walk of life in such
a way that, unless Congress "gets on the bandwagon," it
risks being left behind as an obsolete institution.

The Informing Function

If the use of the Internet after the September 11 terrorist
attacks and the October anthrax crisis helped members,
committees, and staff to carry on their internal operations, it also highlighted that most members were not
prepared to remotely access and respond to their external e-mail communications with constituents at the critical time.

This constituent-informing function is a key aspect of
the democratic communication process. Congress has a
responsibility not only to keep in touch with the concerns and needs of the citizenry, but also to communicate to the public what the government is doing.
That includes communicating information to the people about legislation currently being debated in the
Congress and how representatives vote. Information
technologies in general, and the Internet in particular,

should facilitate the larger, informal public deliberation that should be an important factor in Congress's more formal deliberations.

Moreover, Congress has a responsibility to explain to the people the processes of their government as much as the issues being dealt with through those processes. If the people do not "appreciate and revere the process of deliberation, debate and compromise" as much as they do the issues being debated, said one staff person, then they are likely to become impatient and frustrated with the pace of the process, and to look elsewhere for solutions.

How well is Congress using the new technologies to inform the public? Even though Congress got an early start on the Internet in 1995, with Speaker Newt Gingrich's initiative to establish the Library of Congress's THOMAS Web site, one gets the distinct impression that Congress has not begun to fully grasp what needs to be done to bring congressional deliberation into the twenty-first century.

Perhaps there is no better symbol for this lag-time effect than the Congressional Internet Caucus, an informal, bipartisan group of House and Senate members coming together to learn more and inform their colleagues about Internet issues and legislation. If you tried to find the caucus using the House of Representatives search engine, using the term *Internet,* it would not come up on any of the first 100 (out of 9,291) entries, "ranked by relevance," in the 107th Congress. You would however, turn up a large number of hearings and statements on Internet issues.

If you were fortunate enough to know that the two House co-chairs of the Congressional Internet Caucus are Rep. Rick Boucher (D-Va.) and Rep. Bob Goodlatte (R-Va.), you might have more luck going directly to their House Web pages. Indeed, Rep. Boucher's Web page does direct you to a page for the Congressional Internet Caucus. However, when you click on that link, you end up on a page with the following message: "This page is currently under construction. Please check back soon. Please Visit The Internet Caucus Advisory Committee At <http:// www.netcaucus.org>."[14]

The point is not to embarrass the Congressional Internet Caucus, but rather to highlight just how behind the learning curve even the "Internet leaders" in Congress seem to be. As it turns out, a few members are quite active in their own right on Internet policy issues, as is evident from the hearing testimony presented, legislation introduced, and Internet-related information posted on their individual Web pages. But beyond this, few members are expressing any concern about how this is affecting the institution of Congress and how Congress might use the Internet to change itself to create a better connection between public policy issues, citizens, their government, and elected representatives.

A nonscientific survey of members' Web sites, for instance, turns up only a smattering of representatives who provide links to plain-English information about *how the legislative process works*, or simple *explanations of major pending policy issues and the options for addressing them.* And yet, explaining or providing ready access to process and policy information should be among the most important responsibilities of Congress in assisting the public to be a part of the national deliberative process.

A more detailed survey of all House member Web pages was conducted by the author at two points during the first session of the 107th Congress to assess how well members were communicating their positions on major legislation. The first survey was conducted the week after the March 8, 2001, House vote on the major piece of President Bush's $1.6 trillion tax cut. The second survey was conducted in mid-November on two major votes: the September 14 House vote on the joint resolution (H.J. Res. 64) authorizing the president to use force against those involved with the September 11 terrorist attacks; and the November 1 vote on the initial passage of the so-called aviation security bill (H.R. 3159). Only 28 percent of all members explained their votes on the tax bill; 18 percent, on the use-of-force resolution; and 25 percent, on the aviation security bill (see table 1).

The biggest disparity between the parties is on the tax vote, with 39 percent of Republicans explaining their votes, but only 17 percent of Democrats. It stands to reason that members are more likely to explain something they support—in this case, a modified version of a Republican president's tax bill—than to tell why they voted against it and for an alternative Democratic substitute that lost. The use-of-force data are more difficult to understand since the resolution was overwhelmingly adopted, 410 to 1. It may be that members didn't explain it because it was such a large, favorable vote. However, that would not explain why a larger percent-

Table 1. House Member Web Pages That Did and Did Not Explain Members' Positions on Initial Passage of Three Major Bills in the 107th Congress, 1st Sess. (2001)

Legislation	Democrats: Numbers and (%-D)		Republicans: Numbers and (%-R)		Total Nos. MC	% MC Yes	% MC No
	Yes	No	Yes	No			
Tax bill	37 (17%)	175 (83%)	86 (39%)	135 (61%)	433	28%	72%
Use of force	37 (17%)	175 (83%)	42 (19%)	179 (81%)	433	18%	82%
Aviation security	45 (21%)	167 (79%)	62 (28%)	159 (72%)	433	25%	75%

age of members did have explanations on their Web sites of their votes for the $40 billion emergency spending bill for disaster recovery assistance and antiterrorist defense initiatives, which passed the House on the same day by a vote of 422 to 0.

The low number of Web postings on the aviation security bill is easier to understand since a Democratic substitute narrowly lost, 214 to 218, and the final passage vote on the committee version was 286 to 139. The biggest sticking point was the controversy over whether all airport security personnel (baggage screeners) should be federal employees. Although opinion polls showed popular majorities favoring full federalization of airport security, public opinion has a way of shifting, and therefore many members preferred to wait until the differences between the House and Senate bill were resolved. Indeed, a much larger portion of members hailed the final compromise that was signed into law by the president. Bipartisanship provides political cover and security.

While an increasing number of congressional committees are putting more information on their Web sites, most people don't get beyond their own representative's site—if they get that far. Even then, committees often give summaries of pending or reported bills without offering a broader explanation of the policy issue context. Members and committees could easily remedy this problem by making available on their sites the "issue briefs" prepared by the Congressional Research Service (CRS) at the Library of Congress. But because the CRS is prohibited from making its products available to anyone but members of Congress, few members release the materials on their Web pages. One member, freshman representative Mark Green (R-Wis.), has posted an index and link to all currently active CRS issue briefs and reports.[15]

Another notable exception to the inaccessibility of CRS reports is the Web site of the House Rules Committee, which includes brief explanations of various aspects of the legislative process, plus a large number of CRS issue briefs and longer background papers on everything from committees and the budget process to bicameral differences between the House and Senate, and relations between the president and the Congress.[16]

During his 2000 presidential bid, activist Ralph Nader proposed that members of Congress be required to post their full voting records on their Web sites. While neither the proposal nor the Nader candidacy received much public support, the elevation of the issue in a presidential campaign helped highlight the paucity of robust Web pages. Member Web pages are more likely to contain information on grants for congressional district projects the member is able to bring home than to post details of a member's voting record. For the enterprising and adept constituent Web surfer, of course, there is a way to find members' votes through the Library of Congress's THOMAS Web site. However, there is no search engine that searches the voting data either by issue or by member, let alone by both at once. Moreover, if one were to learn that the Democrats offered an alternative on the aviation security bill, and managed to find that vote on THOMAS, there is no accompanying explanation of the amendment. Instead, the heading above the votes reads simply, "Oberstar of Minnesota Substitute Amendment."[17] Congress and its members have a long way to go if they are to make their presence on the Internet more user-friendly to the average citizen.

The Legislative Possibilities

Closely entangled with Congress's informing function is the use of new communication technologies to assist members with committee and floor work. This raises two key issues: how fast and efficient should the legislative process be, given the inherent slowness of deliberation? How much can or should Congress simultaneously share electronically with the public during the course of its deliberations?

These are some of the important issues raised by a Congressional Research Service report prepared for the House Rules Committee's 21st Century Congress Project, released in 1999. Not surprisingly, the report concluded that the application of technology "has the potential to significantly impact the legislative processes."[18]

One of the striking conclusions is the finding that moving toward an electronic document system in Congress and its committees will probably mean "reduced time for the deliberation process." As the report elaborates: "The use of computers makes it possible to put draft material into a format that appears to be 'final' very rapidly. Yet the appearance of a correctly formatted document may mask the fact that there has been little time to analyze or validate the content. . . . As legislative text moves more seamlessly from initial drafts through final publication, one loses the time between each stage of the process that historically has been available for further consideration of the wording and for performing quality control."[19]

This prospect of instant, electronic availability of evolving bill text and proposed amendments in committee or on the floor raises the larger question of whether the same materials should be made available to the public simultaneously over the Internet, as some public interest groups have strongly urged.[20] As the CRS report notes, "the time gaps that traditionally have existed as drafts were revised, bills marked up and committee reports prepared—time which is often used to reach compromises, eliminate errors, and consider alternatives—may be lost if electronic versions of bills are rapidly composed and placed on web sites. Conversely, increased public exposure to the process may permit citizen input to be more directly considered during committee deliberations."[21]

The report goes on to offer a potpourri of electronic possibilities that Congress might utilize in its committees, from electronic briefing books for hearings and markups to "virtual" markups and reporting of bills using networked systems, including remote, electronic voting.[22]

The report revisits the issue of whether members should be allowed to bring their own laptop computers onto the floor of the House and Senate. This practice had been informally rejected by both the House and the Senate rules committees, on grounds that it would detract from the dignity, decorum, and integrity of the deliberations in the two chambers.[23] Among the questions raised by a CRS report on the subject, which provided both pros and cons on the floor use of laptops, were (1) whether members would be inundated with e-mail from lobbyists and constituents during actual floor debate; (2) whether members would have better access to information that could make a positive contribution to the deliberations under way; and (3) whether the presence of laptops might sacrifice collegiality to efficiency.[24]

As with the prospect of remote committee voting, the 1999 CRS report speculated on the possibility of remote floor voting using any number of options for ensuring security and authentication, from digital signatures to biometric verification (digital fingerprints or retinal scans). Putting all these possibilities together, the report concluded that "in the future, one might be able to convene a 'virtual' House and conduct votes without Members being physically present." But it added that "there seems to be little support among Members . . . for the idea of voting remotely and strong sentiment in favor of coming together to debate and vote on legislation."[25]

Coalitions and Polling

Other issues include the ability of members to more easily form ad hoc groups to promote a cause, bill, or amendment; the effects such member-to-member communication have on the leadership's ability to hold party members together; the increasing use of information technologies by outside interest groups to mobilize their memberships for legislative purposes; and the growing adeptness and frequency of constituents in using e-mail to contact members on pending legislation.[26]

Given these converging factors, the CRS report asked how these trends will affect members torn between conflicting constituent and national interests; how online polling of constituents by members will affect a member's position on an issue; whether the new communication possibilities will weaken allegiance to party leadership; and whether the ability of constituents and interest groups to observe members acting in real time will affect members' abilities to develop compromises and experiment with new approaches.[27]

The possibility, cited above, of members using their Web pages to conduct polling of their constituents on pending matters was raised in another and earlier committee report. In 1997 a subgroup of the House Oversight (now House Administration) Committee reported to the full committee on the "cyber" accomplishments of the 104th Congress.[28]

In its report, the working group noted that House Web sites were becoming "increasingly more attractive and innovative," and that members and comittees were experimenting with the technology "to develop new ways to communicate with and empower the citizens of our nation." Such empowerment includes enabling citizens to "be better informed about legislative and legal issues," and facilitating communication between them and their elected officials."

One of the examples cited in the report of how the twin aims of legislative information and communication could be joined through the Internet was "conducting electronic surveys using interactive sites," among other things, "to find out how constituents would vote on *pending* legislation [emphasis added]."[29]

Conclusions

Notwithstanding these efforts by the House Rules and House Oversight Committees, there has been little follow-up work done on the implications and options presented in the two reports. As of the beginning of the 107th Congress in 2001, the 21st Century Congress Project Web page had been removed from the Rules Committee's site (thought it has since reappeared on the Web page of the committee's recently renamed Subcommittee on Technology and the House).[30] The House Oversight Committee's Computer and Information Services Working Group was not reconstituted in either the 106th or the 107th Congresses (though many of its recommendations have been implemented by the Chief Administrative Officer through House Information Resources [HIR]). It is true, with each passing year, that the information and capabilities of the House, Senate, and THOMAS Web sites continue to expand and improve.

But what is missing from this technological progress is some clear vision shared by members of the House and Senate of what the relationship should be between the new information technologies and the core lawmaking and representational functions of the Congress.

One should not be too surprised that Congress does not now see any of this as a possible problem for our representative democracy, and that it does not have a pro-active approach to addressing the subject. One thing that has remained relatively constant about the institution over the years is that it is a reactive rather than a pro-active body, and usually does not act until a crisis occurs.

In the meantime, to the extent that anyone is paying attention to this problem within the institution, it is the "techies" who will likely set the course in the absence of direction from above or from the whole. This includes the management of HIR, the staff members of the House and Senate administration committees who are literate in information technology, and the "systems administrators" in member, committee, and leadership offices. It may also include a few computer-literate members of Congress. But their chances of involving their more technologically challenged colleagues in the larger questions of such an enterprise are negligible.

Does it really matter whether members actually confront the implications of the information age, as long as there is willing, committed, and competent staff to look after the technical details? Won't things just naturally evolve, given capable staff guidance, to meet the needs of the times?

Increased staff expertise alone does not appear to be enough. The Stennis Fellows called for the creation of House and Senate short-term special committees on information technology and congressional deliberation, patterned after the recent Senate Special Committee on the Y2K Problem. The committees would "explore needed institutional changes (innovations) to strengthen congressional deliberation with information technology." This exercise would produce "some champions among members" for the cause of ensuring that information technology development promotes better deliberation, in the broader sense of greater involvement of the public in the policy process, without destroying the ultimate responsibility of Congress to make the final deliberative decisions.[31]

And therein lies the conundrum. Is it possible for Congress to allow real-time public awareness of, and participation in, a process that requires sufficient time and space for Congress to develop the necessary compromises for a national policy consensus that is acceptable both internally and externally? Two political scientists captured the essence of this congressional conundrum in an essay titled "Deliberation: An Untimed Value in a Timed Game."[32] Their work was published before the Internet was even a factor in the deliberative process. The authors' historic overview demonstrates how the decline of deliberation in Congress has been inversely proportional to the growth in the number and complexity of issues with which it has had to deal, meaning that there is less time available to deliberate on each.

The computer and information services working group of the House Oversight Committee offered the following comments on how the new computer technologies are the culmination of the founders' intentions: "Although the Founding Fathers could not have foreseen the technology that would give rise to the Cyber-Congress initiative, they would have readily understood the value of its implementation. Communication is the very essence of representative democracy. The empowerment of the citizen through computer-mediated communication technologies is the focus of [Speaker Gingrich's] vision. While it promises to usher in a new era of informed citizen participation in the business of the

House, it is not a new idea, but rather the realization of the full potential for representative democracy envisioned by the founding Fathers at the Constitutional Convention two centuries ago."[33]

This is not incompatible with something Madison wrote back in 1822, when he observed that "[a] popular Government, without popular information, or the means of acquiring it, is but a Prologue to a Farce or a Tragedy; or perhaps both." And he went on, "Knowledge will forever govern ignorance: And a people who mean to be their own Governors must arm themselves with the power which knowledge gives.[34]

How much citizen knowledge and participation is a logical extension of the founders' intent? In advocating two-year terms for House members, according to one constitutional scholar, the Federalists recognized that "for the whole process to work, members must look forward and deliberate with each other—an impossibility if every moment is spent looking over the shoulder at the home constituency."[35] As Alexander Hamilton put it, in arguing for longer terms during the constitutional convention's debates, "There ought to be neither too much nor too little dependence on the popular sentiments."[36]

Are we nearing the point at which internal deliberation may be made impossible in Congress because external participation is both continuous and overwhelming? There can be no question that the information super-highway can further arm the people with the knowledge that will enable them to better govern themselves through their elected representatives. However,

just because the information super-highway and deliberation are both two-way streets does not mean that
they are perfectly integrated and compatible systems. In
reality, they operate at radically different speeds. If the
information super-highway is not used to enhance both
congressional deliberation and citizen involvement in a
balanced manner, our system of deliberative democracy
may well become a relic.

That is the challenge Congress will have to face, or
to ignore at its peril, in the next few years. Will it travel
the path of least resistance—that is, go with the electronic flow that promotes the greatest convenience,
efficiency, and self-preservation for members through
constituent service and reelection efforts, while merely
processing public opinion polls into public laws? Or
will it still make time for the much less efficient, more
time-consuming, and politically perilous path of deliberative lawmaking? Put another way, will Congress recognize that e-liberation is not the same as deliberation,
and that House and Senate committee and chamber debates cannot be replaced by cyber-polling and chatroom
exchanges?

Madison left no doubt as to the position he would
take on this question. For him, it would be the simple
choice between a pure democracy driven by popular
passions at the expense of minority and property rights
(and thus doomed to a short life and violent death), and
a republic in which public opinion is refined and en-
larged through the medium of an elected body of citizens "whose wisdom may best discern the true interest
of their country."[37]

Notes

Parts of this chapter are based on a paper presented at a conference on "Congress, the Internet, and Deliberative Democracy," held in Washington, D.C., 4 May 2001, and published in *Congress and the Internet,* ed. James A. Thurber and Colton C. Campbell (Upper Saddle River, N.J.: Prentice Hall, 2002).

1. The roundtable discussion held at the Wilson Center on 22 January 2001, on "The Information Age Congress and Deliberation: A Staff Perspective," was an outgrowth of the John C. Stennis Center's Congressional Fellowship Program in the 106th Congress (1999–2000), which brought together twenty-eight senior House and Senate staff members from both parties. The group's final discussion paper, "Congress Meets the Information Age: Deliberation in the 21st Century," questioned whether Congress could keep pace with the tempo of the information age. Three of the Stennis Fellows summarized their class's report and then joined in a further discussion of the topic with area political scientists, other congressional staff persons, and Fellows from the Wilson Center.

2. "BlackBerry Envy," news item found on the Congress Online Project's electronic newsletter, 13 November 2001, at <html://www.congressonlineproject.org/November.html>.

3. Helen Dewar, "Lawmakers Want Their Mail Back; Stoppage Disrupts Link to Constituents," *Washington Post*, 28 October 2001, A-17.

4. Ibid.

5. Congress Online Project, electronic newsletter, 2 November 2001, accessed on 14 November 2001, at <http://www.congressonlineproject.org/November.html>.

6. "An Open Letter to the American People from Speaker Hastert and Democratic Leader Gephardt," 26 October 2001, accessed on November 14, 2001, at <http://www.gop.gov/itemnews.asp?N=20011026155442>.

7. Web page of "Bill Frist, M.D.," accessed on 14 November 2002, at <http://www.senate.gov/~frist/>.

8. Eliza Newlin Carney, "E-mail Increases on Hill; Lawmakers Not Equipped to Respond," *National Journal's Congress Daily AM*, 2 November 2001, 8.

9. John C. Stennis Congressional Staff Fellows, 106th Congress, "Congress Meets the Information Age: Deliberation in the 21st Century: A Discussion Paper," unpublished final draft, 25 September 2000, 13.

10. Ibid.

11. Ibid, 14.

12. The summary presentations of the group's discussion paper were delivered by Rochelle Dornant, chief of staff to Rep. Sam Farr (D-Calif.); Robert Simon, Democratic staff director of the Senate Energy and Natural Resources Committee; and Kristine Iverson, legislative director to Senator Orrin Hatch (R-Utah). To encourage a frank discussion, the roundtable was off the record, so no quotations will be attributed here to any of the participants by name.

13. "E-mail Overload in Congress: Managing a Communications Crisis," a report of the Congress Online Project, funded by a grant from the Pew Charitable Trusts, accessed on 19 March 2001, at <http://www.congressonlineproject.org/email.html>.

14. Accessed on 13 February 2001, at <http://www.house.gov/boucher/underconstruction.htm>.

15. The CRS index page on Rep. Mark Green's Web site can be accessed at: <http://www.house.gov/markgreen/crs.htm>.

16. See the Rules Committee's Web site at: <http://www.house.gov/rules/welcome.htm>.

17. "Final Vote Results for Roll Call 423, H.R. 3150, Nov. 1, 2001, 7:59 p.m., Oberstar of Minnesota Substitute Amendment," rejected, 214 to 218, accessed on 21 November 2001, at <http://clerkweb.house.gov/cgi-bin/vote.exe?year=2001& rollnumber=423 >.

18. Jane Bortnick Griffith, "Information Technology in the House of Representatives: Trends and Potential Impact on Legislative Process," a report prepared for the House Committee on Rules by the Congressional Research Service, 1999, 1, formerly found at: <http://www.house.gov:80/rules/infotech99.htm>.

19. Ibid., 9.

20. See, for instance, Gary Ruskin (director of the Congressional Accountability Project) and Kenneth R. Weinstein, "Congress Is Plugged-In; Now It must Increase Access to Information," *Roll Call,* 9 December 1996. At the beginning of the 105th Congress in 1997, the House did adopt a new rule that reads, "Each committee shall make its publications available in electronic form to the maximum extent feasible" (now House Rule XI, clause 2(e)(4)). This does not address the demand by some that committee amendments and chairmen's marks be posted on the Internet contemporaneously with their consideration in committee, since these are not considered committee publications (i.e., printed documents available to the public). Under House Rules, a committee report is not an official document until it is filed with the clerk. That is not to say, however, that prior publication of a substitute bill as a "committee print" is prohibited. Many committees already publish such documents for the use of members, staff, and the public during committee markups of bills.

21. Bortnick Griffith, "Information Technology in the House of Representatives," 12.

22. Ibid.

23. See, for instance, Walter J. Oleszek and Jane Bortnick Griffith, "Electronic Devices in the House Chamber," Congressional Research Service Report, 21 November 1997. At the beginning of the 106th Congress in 1997, the House adopted a rule that reads: "A person may not smoke or use any personal, electronic office equipment, including cellular phones and computers, on the floor of the House" (now House Rule XVII, clause 5). The rule was initially prompted by members' receiving and making cellular phone calls in the House Chamber, though the future prospect of requests to bring personal computers was also contemplated by the rule's prohibition. The Senate has no specific rule banning personal computers on the floor, but the practice is prohibited under the general rules of decorum in the absence of a rule authorizing their use.

24. Bortnick Griffith, "Information Technology in the House of Representatives," 13.

25. Ibid.

26. Ibid., 14–15.

27. Ibid., 15.

28. "CyberCongress Accomplishments during the 104th Congress," a report of the Computer and Information Services Working Group to the Committee on House Oversight, 11 February 1997, accessed in January 2000, at <http://www.house.gov:80/cha/publications/publications.html>.

29. Ibid., 6–7 (emphasis added).

30. Accessed on 21 November 2001, at <http://www.house.gov/rules/sub_th_21century.htm>.

31. Stennis Congressional Staff Fellows discussion paper, 16–17.

32. George E. Connor and Bruce I. Oppenheimer, "Deliberation: An Untimed Value in a Timed Game," in *Congress Reconsidered*, ed. Lawrence C. Dodd and Bruce I. Oppenheimer, 5th ed. (Washington, D.C.: CQ Press, 1993), chap. 13, 315–330.

33. "CyberCongress Accomplishments," 10.

34. Madison to William T. Barry, 4 August 1822, in *James Madison: Writings*, ed. Jack N. Rakove (New York: Literary Classics of the United States, 1999), 790.

35. Connor and Oppenheimer, "Deliberation: An Untimed Value in a Timed Game," 318, quoting from Michael J. Malbin.

36. "Debates in the Federal Convention of 1787 as Reported by James Madison," 21 June 1787, in *Documents Illustrative of the Formation of the Union of the American States,* House Doc. 398, 69th Cong., 1st sess. (Washington, D.C.: Government Printing Office, 1927), 256.

37. Alexander Hamilton, James Madison, and John Jay, *The Federalist Papers*, No. 10 (New York: New American Library of World Literature, Mentor Books, 1962), 82.

 # Conclusion

Leslie David Simon

The Internet's technological and institutional forebears—
printing, postal service, telephones, broadcasting, and
computers—have been used for both good and evil. But
while the enemies of democracy have used all of these
with varying degrees of success, over time each of these
innovations inexorably helped to modernize societies
around the world and accelerate the growth of democracy. The potential that each offered for facilitating
communications between ever-widening circles of people, for spreading information, and for nurturing education far overpowered the attempts of totalitarians to
use them as tools of repression.

While our decade-long experience with the Internet is
more limited, we can already begin to discern the same
patterns, although with differing effects and issues in
different countries. Moreover, the Internet adds some
new dimensions, especially its robust facilitation of the
right of association and its global reach.

However, the degree to which the Internet facilitates
democracy varies greatly. Strong democracies like the

United States, the nations of the European Union, Canada, and others are making the most of it. Fledgling democracies that also tend to be poorer nations are beginning to make some gains, particularly in the areas of civil society and education. The most repressive regimes do their best to keep the democratizing influences at bay, but face a constant challenge as dissidents attempt to use the Internet. The poorest and most strife-ridden countries, like those of sub-Saharan Africa, are not yet in the game.

In a strong democracy like the United States, the early fears expressed by some that the use of the Internet would result in government by instant referendum and the breakdown of representative democracy have not materialized. On the contrary, the recent experience of the U.S. Congress following the events of September 11, 2001, shows that representative democracy can be strengthened by the Internet, even in times of great stress to democratic institutions. The Internet not only helped Congress to continue its operations in the months after the attacks, even as congressional office buildings remained closed, but it facilitated on-going communications between members of Congress and their constituents.

Congress now needs to capitalize on its tenuous Internet advances and develop a clear vision for the future. As Donald Wolfensberger has pointed out in chapter 3, among the questions it needs to answer are the following: Should all of Congress's operations—markups, internal elections, hearings, legislative drafts—be exposed on the Internet? Should Congress permit laptop computers on the floor and allow remote voting by members?

Should congressional Web sites be used to poll constituents? Congress should answer these questions itself, before de facto answers are imposed on it.

Moreover, Congress needs to look at the Net not as an appendage to existing ways of conducting itself, but as a means of reinventing itself. Businesses have learned that the really important benefits of the Net come not from using it to run traditional operations, but from using it as a tool to reorganize and revitalize themselves. For example, the Internet can be used by companies to purchase materials by soliciting bids. This saves companies money and time. But some companies go a step further and use the Net to organize online competitions where would-be suppliers bid against each other, thereby gaining real competitive advantage. Congress needs to view the Internet in the same creative way.

In weaker democracies, like those in much of Latin America, the ability of citizens to harness the Internet for democratic purposes can be seen today in a variety of ways. In particular, the earliest beneficiaries of the Internet have been nongovernmental organizations, political parties, and other institutions of civil society. Clearly, in Latin America the Internet is empowering individual citizens and democratic institutions far more than it can empower authoritarian regimes.

However, as Javier Corrales has shown in chapter 2, the greatest barrier to the Internet's democratizing potential is the limited access to it that citizens have, for a variety of reasons. While market forces are a prerequisite for the broad diffusion of the Internet, the market alone cannot create universal access in regions like Latin

America. A concerted effort will be needed by the private sector, government, and the educational establishment to bring the Internet to everyone—especially to low-income and poorly educated groups. This can be accomplished by providing free or low-cost access in public spaces, such as schools, government buildings, community centers, and libraries. One can already observe this phenomenon in places like San Miguel de Allende in the state of Guanajuato, Mexico, where a co-operative community effort has placed Internet connections in the public library.

But can the Internet illuminate even those regions of the world that are the least democratic and the least free? In the Middle East, for example, we see not only the economic difficulties that hinder growth of the Internet in poor countries, such as Egypt and Jordan. We also see some of the strongest government reactions against the Internet from regimes that obviously fear it—even in rich countries like Saudi Arabia, where in theory the cost of access should be no barrier. Nevertheless, I believe the Internet can wield a positive influence in this part of the world, although not in every country, and not without some assistance from the democracies.

First, as I showed in chapter 1, the basic characteristics of the Internet (or the Net, as I refer to the broader phenomenon) help to enable democracy and democratic institutions. Wherever it operates, even with forms of censorship and regulation, the Internet still beams some democratic light into repressive darkness. Second, absent almost total repression of the type that is found in Iraq, dictators always play catch-up with technology. Citizens find ways around regulations and censors

Third, the economic imperatives of the Net are pushing repressive governments to accept its use in one form or another, whether to promote export industries, to lower the cost of government services, or to generally increase productivity throughout the economy. Governments that ignore these economics will grow progressively weaker economically and will find it more difficult to maintain their hold on power. They will become increasingly vulnerable to opposition forces from within and without.

The industrial democracies can help. What should they do? First, through bilateral and multilateral aid programs, they should help countries build Net infrastructure and help them work toward universal access. A wide variety of programs already exist, such as those sponsored by the World Bank, the G-8, and the United Nations Development Program. Regional organizations, such as APEC and the OAS, should also step up their activities. These organizations can provide training for professionals; develop applications in critical areas such as health care, education, job placement, and food distribution; and provide funding and expertise to build testbeds for public access systems. Even the poorest countries can benefit from such programs, as World Bank efforts in impoverished nations in Africa already show.

Second, the democracies must raise the international temperature to protect free expression and the natural openness of the global Net. While the protection of freedom of speech and association in their own countries is the *sine qua non*, they must also hammer away at every international forum possible on these protections around the world. There is no shortage of venues. Examples of existing international agreements that cover freedom of expression include the U.N. Universal Declaration of Human Rights; the International Covenant on Civil and Political Rights (ratified by 140 nations); and the International Covenant on Economic, Social and Cultural Rights (ratified by 136 nations). There are also key regional agreements, such as the European Convention of Human Rights; the American Declaration of the Rights and Duties of Man and the American Convention on Human Rights; and the African Charter on Human and Peoples' Rights. Despite the Orwellian politicization and distortion of human rights at the United Nations in recent years, as evidenced at its failed 2001 Durban Conference, the democracies must mount an offensive against censorship and other regulations and laws that restrict Net freedom.

There are still those who fear that the Internet will be hemmed in ultimately by borders just as the physical world is. They cite not only the work of the dictators, but also growing national restrictions on Net activities that reflect national practice in areas such as gambling, advertising, or selling pharmaceuticals. Undoubtedly, countries will protect their legitimate national interests in areas ranging from protecting children from pedophiles to ensuring the presence of their national language and culture on the Net. None of these activities needs to erode the Net's inherent support of democracy, however. On the contrary, to the extent that they reassure people that their beliefs and customs can be respected in the virtual world, they can increase the acceptance of the Net by more people.

We are just at the beginning of the Internet's invasion of the world's institutions. Only time will tell who will win the race between freedom and oppression. My bet is that the Internet adds a nice breeze behind the sails of democracy.

✍ Index

Note: Page numbers followed by *f*, *t*, or *n* indicate figures, tables, or notes respectively.

A

access issues, cell phone subscribers, 42*t*; have-nots, 35–36; Latin America, x, 38, 41, 42*t*, 49*f*; Middle East, 16–17, 25, 99; North America, 41; poorest nations, 97; rich and poor countries, 6–7; Sub-Saharan Africa, 97; variability, 32; vs. usage, 37
accountability, 35; vs. usage, 37
Afghanistan, Internet banned, 1; type of state, 22
Al Qaeda, 24
anonymizer devices, 35
anthrax scare, xi, 69–73
Apple Computers, 4
Arab governments, ix
Arabic Internet Names Consortium, 17
Arab-Israeli conflict, 24
Argentina, 39–40, 45, 50–51
Authoritarian/repressive regimes, 99–100; alternatives, 27; contradictory Net policy, 14–16; control of Internet use, viii, 2; dissident use of Net, 97; economic motives, 100; effect on technological innovation, 1; electronic government, 12; expansion of Internet, 33; fears of Internet, 54, 57; incentives for expansion,54; Latin America, 33; Middle East, 24; monitoring dissidents, 36; private sector Net involvement, 11; use of Internet, vii
authority, erosion of, 13
aviation security bill, 79, 80*t*, 81
Azerbaijan, 56*t*, 57

B

Bahrain, 16–18
bargaining power, 48
Bell, Daniel, 3
Bin Laden, Osama, 36
BlackBerries, 69–73
borders, cyberspace, 10; erosion of, 8–9; on Internet, 101–2
Brand, Stewart, 4
Brazil, 38, 43–45; Internet expansion, 56*t*, 57
Bush, George W., 34

C

Canada, 41
capitalism, 6
cellular phones, 38, 94n
censorship, democracies, vii, 7;
    Gulf states, 17; international
    agreements, 101; Iran, 21;
    Middle East, 22–24; Saudi
    Arabia, 19; Turkey, 19
Chávez, Hugo, 39
checks and balances, 11
Chiapas rebellion, 40
Chile, 41, 46; Internet
    expansion, 56t, 57
China, conflicts in Net policy,
    15; government restrictions,
    37; imprisonment policy, viii,
    15; Internet expansion, 56t,
    57; Net control, 15, 23
citizen empowerment, 10, 13,
    86, 89–90
citizens, monitoring abuses, 34;
    types of, 32
civicness, 35
civil society, expanding Internet
    access, 51; Latin America,
    47, 49f, 98; Middle East, 22;
    regime type, 55
Cofetel, 44
communications, patterns, 96;
    systems, 3
computer institutes, 21
computer literacy, 50, 51
computers, 3; pioneers, 4
Congressional Internet Caucus,
    77–78
Congressional Research Service
    (CRS), 81–82, 83
Congress Online Survey project,
    75–76
Congress (U.S.), anthrax
    attacks, 69–73; coalitions
    and polling, 85–86;
constituent-informing
    function, 76–83; deliberation
    issue, 83–85, 88–91;
    informing function, 76–83;
    legislative possibilities,
    83–85; members' Web sites,
    78–79; reactive approach,
    87–88; reinventing itself, 98;
    September 11 impact, 67–69,
    97; two scenarios for
    Internet approach, 73–76;
    universe of technologies, 75;
    visibility as role model, xi
connectivity. See Internet
    connectivity
constituents, communicating
    with, 67, 69–73; e-mail use
    by constituents, 85–86;
    function of Congress, 76–83
consumers, 13
contentious collective action, 48
content issue, free speech limits,
    26; Middle East, 23–24
coordinating agent, need for,
    32–33; incentives, 53–57;
    Internet connectivity, 48,
    50–53; overview, 58–59
Costa Rica, voting online, 13
counterculture of 1960s, 4
Cuba, 56t, 57
cultural content, 13–14
cyber-cafés, Middle East, 17–21
cyber-coalitions, 34, 40

D

Daschle, Tom (Rep.), 68
Defense Department (U.S.), 4,
    26
deliberation issue, 83–85, 88–91
democracy, alternative scenarios
    for U.S. Congress, 73–76;
    representative, 97

democratic development, 31
democratic potential,
    information, 33–35; Internet
    connectivity, 46–48; Middle
    East, 25–27; overview, xi;
    pros and cons, 30–31;
    thwarting, 14–16; variability,
    96–97
democratic states, expansion of
    Internet, 54–55, 57
democratization, authoritarian
    states' dilemma, 54;
    economic liberalization, 47;
    effects and causes, 58; elites-
    first, 47, 49f; Internet
    connectivity, 33–37
developing countries, best sites,
    58; expansion of Internet,
    55, 56t, 57–58
digital divide, 6–7
dissidents, abroad, 17
dot-com potential, 30
Dot Force, 25

E

economic liberalization, 32, 41,
    43; democratization related,
    47
economics, Internet linked to
    crashes, 8
education, enabling, 14;
    expanding Internet access,
    50; human potential, 26–27;
    Latin America, 44–45;
    teacher training, 51
Egypt, 18, 22
e-Jihad, 24
elections, U.S. in 2000, 34
electronic commerce,
    dictatorships, 14–15; Middle
    East, 16; Saudi Arabia, 12;
    Turkey, 18

Electronic Frontier Foundation
    (EFF), 4–5
electronic government, 12
elites-first democratization, 47,
    49f
e-mail traffic, U.S. Congress,
    70–71, 75; by constituents,
    85–86
Emirates Telecommunications
    Corporation, 17
end of the Cold War, Internet
    linked, viii, 5–6
Equatorial Guinea, 56t, 57
Eutelsat, 21
expansion of Internet, factors
    influencing, 32–33;
    fundamental barriers, 58;
    incentives, 53–57; types of
    states and contributing
    factors, 56t, 57–58

F

Federalists, 90
foreign investment, 43
Founding Fathers, 89–90
freedom of association,
    100–101; as characteristic of
    Net, 9–10; as new
    dimension, 96; The Well, 4
free expression, 4, 100–101;
    limits to, 7; private sector
    restraint, 26
free trade organizations, 100
Fujimori, Alberto, 39

G

G-8 (Group of Eight), 25
gay and lesbian community,
    Latin America, 40, 62n
General Accounting Office, 68
Gil Díaz, Francisco, 62n

glasnost, 3
Gore, Al, 34, 60*n*
governments, control issues, 9,
11; controlling content,
Middle East, 22; cost
savings, 12; private sector,
boundaries with, 10;
reinventing themselves, 12;
surveillance of citizens, 7, 56*t*
grassroots mobilization, 34
Great Britain, 65*n*–66*n*
Gulf states, 17–18, 22

H

hackers, 7
Hamilton, Alexander, 90
hate groups, viii
House Information Resources
(HIR), 87
House Oversight (now House
Administration) Committee,
86–87, 89; Computer and
Information Service Working
Group, 87
House Rules Committee, 82;
21st Century Congress
Project, 83, 87
human rights agreements, 101
human rights organizations,
Middle East, vii, 22, 24
hype, Internet, 6

I

imprisonment in China, viii
individual empowerment,
government information, 13;
Internet effect, 10; U.S.
Congress, 86, 89–90
industrial democracies, 100
Infloplaza Project, 51–53,
65*n*–66*n*

information, access to
government online, 12;
congressional staff, 88;
democracy, 33–35;
globalization and power, 27;
nature of, 8–9
information age, international
relations, 13
information super-highway,
90–91
information systems, 3;
technology in Congress,
88–89
intellectual property law, fair
use doctrine, 4–5
Inter-American Development
Bank, 52
intermediate regimes, 31–32;
benefit from Internet, x;
Latin America, 37–38
international agreements, 101
international aid, 100
Internet, characteristics, 8–14;
dark or ugly side, 6–8,
35–36
Internet connectivity,
coordination dilemma, 48,
50–53; defined, 32;
democratic theory, 33–37,
46–48; dual roles, 36;
traditional democratic
practices, 35
Internet Society, 4, 5
Iran, 20–21, 22
Iraq, 21, 22
Islamic world, 16–21;
communication, ix;
democratic development, x;
democratic survey, 2; lessons
about Net, 21–24
Israel, 23, 24
issue briefs, 81–82

J

Jobs, Steve, 4
Jordan, 16, 17–18, 22–23

K

Kuwait, 16, 17

L

labor unions, 9
language use, 16–17
laptop computers, 69, 72,
    84–85
Latin America, intermediate
    regimes, 37–38; overview,
    98–99. *See also individual
    countries*
Lebanon, 18, 22
legislation, bill text, 83–84;
    marking up bills, 84, 94*n*
liberalism, political, 6
Libya, 20, 22
Lipset, Seymour Martin, 6, 34
local communities, 51

M

Madison, James, 90–91
Malaysia, 15, 23
maquiladora plants, 40
marginalized groups, 40
market forces, 58
market reforms, 41, 43–46,
    58–59
Marxism, 3
Mexico, 40, 43–44; cooperative
    efforts, 99;
    telecommunications, 62*n*
Middle East, censorship, 22–23;
    democratic potential, 16–21;
    electronic commerce, 16;
    lessons, 21–24; overview,
    99–100; statistics, 28*n*; types
    of states, 22. *See also
    individual countries*
military spending, 23
Morocco, 19–20, 22
multimedia giant corporations,
    36
Muslim nations, fostering
    democracy, x
Myanmar, 15, 56*t*, 57

N

Nader, Ralph, 35, 60*n*, 82
National Bureau of Science,
    Technology, and Innovation
    (SENACYT, Panama), 52
New Economy, 6, 8
newspaper Web sites, 38, 60*n*
nongovernmental organizations
    (NGOs), 51, 98
North Africa, 20

O

OECD countries, Internet
    revolution, 30–31
oil revenues, 23
Oman, 56*t*, 57

P

Palestinians, 24
Panama, 51–53
Paraguay, 56*t*
Peru, 38–39
Philippines, 62*n*
pluralism, accelerated, 34
policy consensus, 89
political organization, 62*n*
political parties, Latin America,
    38, 98

pornography, Middle East, 17
postal deliveries, 69–70
post-industrial society, 3
poverty, barriers to Internet
    expansion, 57; Latin
    America, 45; market-reforms
    related, 45–46; trends
    studied, 64*n*
President's Commission on
    Protecting Critical
    Infrastructure, 26
printing press, ix
privacy issues, anonymizer
    devices, 35; government
    surveillance of citizens, 7;
    Internet violations, 7;
    public and private sectors,
    25–26
private sector, coordination
    needed, 50; leadership role
    proposed, 11; privacy,
    25–26; security, 26
privatization, 43
professional communications,
    13
propaganda, leveraging, 13–14
Publinet, 20
publisher capacity, vii
purchasing power, 45

Q

Qatar, 18

R

radio broadcasting, ix
regional agreements, 101
regional organizations, 100, 101
remote floor voting, 85
representative democracy, 97
Russia, 13

S

satellite service, 21
Saudi Arabia, 19; electronic
    commerce, 12; Internet
    access, 16, 99
security, 26
September 11 attacks, effect on
    Congress, xi, 67–69, 97;
    Islamic nations, 2;
    legislation, 79, 80*t*, 81
Serbia, 14
Singapore, 15, 23
social class, elites first, 47, 49*f*
social movements, 36
software industry, U.S.
    domination, 5
Solidarity trade union (Poland),
    9
South Africa, correspondence
    universities, 14
South Korea, 56*t*, 57
Soviet Union (former USSR), 3
state, coordinating role, 50–53;
    Internet incentives, 53–57
Stennis Center Congressional
    Staff Fellowship program,
    73–75, 88–89, 92*n*
stock market crash
    (2000–2001), 8
struggle, notion of, 48
Subcommittee on Technology
    and the House, 87
surveys, electronic, 86
Syria, 19, 22

T

Taliban, 1
tax cut legislation, 79, 80*t*
technological investments and
    innovation, 41, 43
technology race, winners, 23

telecommunications, competition, 43–44; Latin America, 39t, 41; Mexico, 62n; Middle East, 16–21
telephone service, 38, 42t, 43, 63n, 94
Teleyemen, 23
Telmex, 43–44
terrorist organizations, 24
THOMAS Web site, 82, 87
Tilly, Charles, 48
torture, 24
totalitarian regimes, freedom of decision making, 11–12
transparency, 11
Tunisia, 20, 22
Tunisian Development Bank, 20
Turkey, 18–19, 22

U

United Arab Emirates (UAE), 16, 17
United States, 41. *See also* Congress (U.S.)
universities, online learning, 14

V

Venezuela, 39, 56t, 57
viruses, 7
vote swapping, 35
voting systems online, 13, 60n
voting turnout, 34

W

Web sites, authoritarian regimes, 2; congressional, 71–72, 78–79, 82, 87; citizen empowerment, 86, 89–90; members' voting records, 82; Latin American newspapers, 38, 60n; THOMAS Web site, 82, 87
The Well, 4
wireless revolution, 61n
World Trade Organization (WTO), 44
World Wide Web, 2
worms, 7

Y

Yemen, 22–23

ABOUT THE CENTER

The Center is the living memorial of the United States of America to the nation's twenty-eighth president, Woodrow Wilson. Congress established the Woodrow Wilson Center in 1968 as an international institute for advanced study, "symbolizing and strengthening the fruitful relationship between the world of learning and the world of public affairs." The Center opened in 1970 under its own board of trustees.

In all its activities the Woodrow Wilson Center is a nonprofit, nonpartisan organization, supported financially by annual appropriations from the Congress, and by the contributions of foundations, corporations, and individuals. Conclusions or opinions expressed in Center publications and programs are those of the authors and speakers and do not necessarily reflect the views of the Center staff, fellows, trustees, advisory groups, or any individuals or organizations that provide financial support to the Center.